The Scott Postage Stamp Checklist series

Many collectors enjoy their philatelic journey through collecting stamps country by country. The Scott Postage Stamp Checklist series is designed to aid collectors in forming such collections. These checklists provide collectors with basic information about postage stamps listed with major numbers in the Scott *Standard Postage Stamp Catalogue*. The country name appears at the top of each page, and each row provides the issue date or year, the Scott number, a description and four checkboxes. The first two boxes are labeled at the top of the page as unused and used. The other two boxes are for collectors to label for other collectible options that can be written in, such as never-hinged or on cover.

Jay Bigalke,
Scott catalog editor-in-chief

ADVERTISING INDEX

ISBN: 978-0-89487-639-4

DATE	SCOTT NO.	DESCRIPTION	UNUSED	USED		
Macao						
1884-85	**1**	5r black				
1884-85	**2**	10r orange				
1884-85	**3**	10r green ('85)				
1884-85	**4**	20r bister				
1884-85	**5**	20r rose ('85)				
1884-85	**6**	25r rose				
1884-85	**7**	25r violet ('85)				
1884-85	**8**	40r blue				
1884-85	**9**	40r yellow ('85)				
1884-85	**10**	50r green				
1884-85	**11**	50r blue ('85)				
1884-85	**12**	80r gray ('85)				
1884-85	**13**	100r red lilac				
1884-85	**14**	200r orange				
1884-85	**15**	300r chocolate				
1884	**16**	80r on 100r lilac				
1885	**17**	5r on 25r rose, perf. 12½ (Bk)				
1885	**18**	10r on 25r rose (Bl)				
1885	**19**	10r on 50r grn, perf. 13½ (Bl)				
1885	**20**	20r on 50r green, perf. 12½ (Bk)				
1885	**21**	40r on 50r grn, perf. 12½ (R)				
1885	**22**	5r on 25r rose (Bk)				
1885	**23**	10r on 50r green (Bk)				
1887	**24**	5r on 80r gray				
1887	**25**	5r on 100r lilac				
1887	**26**	10r on 80r gray				
1887	**27**	10r on 200r orange				
1887	**28**	20r on 80r gray				
1887, Oct. 20	**32**	5r green & buff				
1887, Oct. 20	**33**	10r green & buff				
1887, Oct. 20	**34**	40r green & buff				
1888, Jan.	**35**	5r black				
1888, Jan.	**36**	10r green				
1888, Jan.	**37**	20r rose				
1888, Jan.	**38**	25r violet				

DATE	SCOTT NO.	DESCRIPTION	UNUSED	USED		
Macao						
1888, Jan.	**39**	40r chocolate	☐	☐	☐	☐
1888, Jan.	**40**	50r blue	☐	☐	☐	☐
1888, Jan.	**41**	80r gray	☐	☐	☐	☐
1888, Jan.	**42**	100r brown	☐	☐	☐	☐
1888, Jan.	**43**	200r gray lilac	☐	☐	☐	☐
1888, Jan.	**44**	300r orange	☐	☐	☐	☐
1892	**45**	30r on 200r gray lil	☐	☐	☐	☐
1894, Nov. 15	**46**	5r yellow	☐	☐	☐	☐
1894, Nov. 15	**47**	10r redsh violet	☐	☐	☐	☐
1894, Nov. 15	**48**	15r chocolate	☐	☐	☐	☐
1894, Nov. 15	**49**	20r lavender	☐	☐	☐	☐
1894, Nov. 15	**50**	25r green	☐	☐	☐	☐
1894, Nov. 15	**51**	50r lt blue	☐	☐	☐	☐
1894, Nov. 15	**52**	75r carmine	☐	☐	☐	☐
1894, Nov. 15	**53**	80r yellow green	☐	☐	☐	☐
1894, Nov. 15	**54**	100r brown, buff	☐	☐	☐	☐
1894, Nov. 15	**55**	150r carmine, rose	☐	☐	☐	☐
1894, Nov. 15	**56**	200r dk blue, blue	☐	☐	☐	☐
1894, Nov. 15	**57**	300r dk blue, sal	☐	☐	☐	☐
1894	**58**	1a on 5r black (R)	☐	☐	☐	☐
1894	**59**	3a on 20r car (G)	☐	☐	☐	☐
1894	**60**	4a on 25r violet (Bk)	☐	☐	☐	☐
1894	**61**	6a on 40r choc (Bk)	☐	☐	☐	☐
1894	**62**	8a on 50r blue (R)	☐	☐	☐	☐
1894	**63**	13a on 80r gray (Bk)	☐	☐	☐	☐
1894	**64**	16a on 100r brn (Bk)	☐	☐	☐	☐
1894	**65**	31a on 200r gray lil (Bk)	☐	☐	☐	☐
1894	**66**	47a on 300r org (G)	☐	☐	☐	☐
1894	**66B**	5a on 30r on 200r	☐	☐	☐	☐
1898, Apr. 1	**67**	½a blue green	☐	☐	☐	☐
1898, Apr. 1	**68**	1a red	☐	☐	☐	☐
1898, Apr. 1	**69**	2a red violet	☐	☐	☐	☐
1898, Apr. 1	**70**	4a yellow green	☐	☐	☐	☐
1898, Apr. 1	**71**	8a dark blue	☐	☐	☐	☐
1898, Apr. 1	**72**	12a violet brown	☐	☐	☐	☐
1898, Apr. 1	**73**	16a bister brown	☐	☐	☐	☐
1898, Apr. 1	**74**	24a bister	☐	☐	☐	☐
1898-1903	**75**	½a gray	☐	☐	☐	☐

DATE	SCOTT NO.	DESCRIPTION	UNUSED	USED		
Macao						
1898-1903	**76**	1a orange	☐	☐	☐	☐
1898-1903	**77**	2a yellow green	☐	☐	☐	☐
1898-1903	**78**	2a gray grn ('03)	☐	☐	☐	☐
1898-1903	**79**	2½a red brown	☐	☐	☐	☐
1898-1903	**80**	3a gray violet	☐	☐	☐	☐
1898-1903	**81**	3a slate ('03)	☐	☐	☐	☐
1898-1903	**82**	4a sea green	☐	☐	☐	☐
1898-1903	**83**	4a carmine ('03)	☐	☐	☐	☐
1898-1903	**84**	5a gray brn ('00)	☐	☐	☐	☐
1898-1903	**85**	5a pale yel brn ('03)	☐	☐	☐	☐
1898-1903	**86**	6a red brn ('03)	☐	☐	☐	☐
1898-1903	**87**	8a blue	☐	☐	☐	☐
1898-1903	**88**	8a gray brn ('03)	☐	☐	☐	☐
1898-1903	**89**	10a sl bl ('00)	☐	☐	☐	☐
1898-1903	**90**	12a rose	☐	☐	☐	☐
1898-1903	**91**	12a red lil ('03)	☐	☐	☐	☐
1898-1903	**92**	13a violet	☐	☐	☐	☐
1898-1903	**93**	13a gray lilac ('03)	☐	☐	☐	☐
1898-1903	**94**	15a pale ol grn ('00)	☐	☐	☐	☐
1898-1903	**95**	16a dk blue, bl	☐	☐	☐	☐
1898-1903	**96**	18a org brn, pink ('03)	☐	☐	☐	☐
1898-1903	**97**	20a brn, yelsh ('00)	☐	☐	☐	☐
1898-1903	**98**	24a brown, buff	☐	☐	☐	☐
1898-1903	**99**	31a red lilac	☐	☐	☐	☐
1898-1903	**100**	31a red lil, pink ('03)	☐	☐	☐	☐
1898-1903	**101**	47a dk blue, rose	☐	☐	☐	☐
1898-1903	**102**	47a dull bl, straw ('03)	☐	☐	☐	☐
1898-1903	**103**	78a blk & red, bl ('00)	☐	☐	☐	☐
1900	**104**	5a on 13a violet	☐	☐	☐	☐
1900	**105**	10a on 16a dk bl, bl	☐	☐	☐	☐
1900	**106**	15a on 24a brn, buff	☐	☐	☐	☐
1900	**107**	20a on 31a red lilac	☐	☐	☐	☐
1902	**108**	6a on 10r orange	☐	☐	☐	☐
1902	**109**	6a on 10r green	☐	☐	☐	☐
1902	**110**	6a on 5r black	☐	☐	☐	☐
1902	**111**	6a on 10r green	☐	☐	☐	☐
1902	**112**	6a on 40r choc	☐	☐	☐	☐
1902	**113**	18a on 20r rose	☐	☐	☐	☐

DATE	SCOTT NO.	DESCRIPTION	UNUSED	USED		
Macao						
1902	**114**	18a on 25r violet	☐	☐	☐	☐
1902	**115**	18a on 80r gray	☐	☐	☐	☐
1902	**116**	18a on 100r brown	☐	☐	☐	☐
1902	**117**	18a on 200r gray lil	☐	☐	☐	☐
1902	**118**	18a on 300r orange	☐	☐	☐	☐
1902-10	**119**	6a on 5r yellow	☐	☐	☐	☐
1902-10	**120**	6a on 10r red vio	☐	☐	☐	☐
1902-10	**121**	6a on 15r choc	☐	☐	☐	☐
1902-10	**122**	6a on 25r green	☐	☐	☐	☐
1902-10	**123**	6a on 80r yel grn	☐	☐	☐	☐
1902-10	**124**	6a on 100r brn, buff, perf 13½	☐	☐	☐	☐
1902-10	**125**	6a on 200r bl, bl	☐	☐	☐	☐
1902-10	**126**	18a on 20r lavender	☐	☐	☐	☐
1902-10	**127**	18a on 50r lt blue	☐	☐	☐	☐
1902-10	**128**	18a on 75r carmine	☐	☐	☐	☐
1902-10	**129**	18a on 150r car, rose	☐	☐	☐	☐
1902-10	**130**	18a on 300r bl, sal	☐	☐	☐	☐
1902-10	**131**	18a on 2½r brown	☐	☐	☐	☐
1902	**132**	2a yellow green	☐	☐	☐	☐
1902	**133**	4a sea green	☐	☐	☐	☐
1902	**134**	8a blue	☐	☐	☐	☐
1902	**135**	10a slate blue	☐	☐	☐	☐
1902	**136**	12a rose	☐	☐	☐	☐
1905	**141**	10a on 12a red lilac	☐	☐	☐	☐
1910, Oct.	**144**	½a gray green	☐	☐	☐	☐
1910, Oct.	**145**	1a yellow green	☐	☐	☐	☐
1910, Oct.	**146**	2a slate	☐	☐	☐	☐
1911, Apr. 2	**147**	½a gray	☐	☐	☐	☐
1911, Apr. 2	**147B**	1a orange	☐	☐	☐	☐
1911, Apr. 2	**148**	2a gray green	☐	☐	☐	☐
1911, Apr. 2	**149**	3a slate	☐	☐	☐	☐
1911, Apr. 2	**150**	4a carmine (G)	☐	☐	☐	☐
1911, Apr. 2	**151**	5a pale yel brn	☐	☐	☐	☐
1911, Apr. 2	**152**	6a red brown	☐	☐	☐	☐
1911, Apr. 2	**153**	8a gray brown	☐	☐	☐	☐
1911, Apr. 2	**154**	10a slate blue	☐	☐	☐	☐
1911, Apr. 2	**155**	13a gray lilac	☐	☐	☐	☐

DATE	SCOTT NO.	DESCRIPTION	UNUSED	USED		
Macao						
1911, Apr. 2	**156**	16a dk blue, bl	☐	☐	☐	☐
1911, Apr. 2	**157**	18a org brn, pink	☐	☐	☐	☐
1911, Apr. 2	**157A**	20a brown, straw	☐	☐	☐	☐
1911, Apr. 2	**157B**	31a red lil, pink	☐	☐	☐	☐
1911, Apr. 2	**157C**	47a dull bl, straw	☐	☐	☐	☐
1911, Apr. 2	**157D**	78a blk & red, bl	☐	☐	☐	☐
1911	**158**	1a on 5r brn & buff	☐	☐	☐	☐
1911	**159**	2a on half of 4a car	☐	☐	☐	☐
1911	**159C**	5a on half of 10a sl bl (#89)	☐	☐	☐	☐
1911	**160**	5a on half of 10a sl bl (#89)	☐	☐	☐	☐
1911	**161**	5a on half of 10a sl bl (#135)	☐	☐	☐	☐
1911	**162**	1a black	☐	☐	☐	☐
1911	**163**	2a black	☐	☐	☐	☐
1913	**164**	6a on 10r grn (R)	☐	☐	☐	☐
1913	**165**	6a on 5r black (G)	☐	☐	☐	☐
1913	**166**	6a on 10r grn (R)	☐	☐	☐	☐
1913	**167**	6a on 40r choc (R)	☐	☐	☐	☐
1913	**168**	18a on 20r car (G)	☐	☐	☐	☐
1913	**169**	18a on 100r brn (R)	☐	☐	☐	☐
1913	**170**	18a on 300r org (R)	☐	☐	☐	☐
1913	**171**	6a on 10r red vio (G)	☐	☐	☐	☐
1913	**172**	6a on 10r red vio (R)	☐	☐	☐	☐
1913	**173**	6a on 15r choc (R)	☐	☐	☐	☐
1913	**174**	6a on 25r grn (R)	☐	☐	☐	☐
1913	**175**	6a on 80r yel grn (R)	☐	☐	☐	☐
1913	**176**	6a on 100r brn, buff (R), buff, perf. 13½ (R)	☐	☐	☐	☐
1913	**177**	18a on 20r lav (R)	☐	☐	☐	☐
1913	**178**	18a on 50r lt bl (R)	☐	☐	☐	☐
1913	**179**	18a on 75r car (G)	☐	☐	☐	☐
1913	**180**	18a on 150r car, rose (G)	☐	☐	☐	☐
1913	**181**	18a on 300r dk bl, sal (R)	☐	☐	☐	☐
1913	**182**	10a on 12a red lil (R)	☐	☐	☐	☐
1913	**183**	2a on 18a on 20r (R)	☐	☐	☐	☐
1913	**184**	2a on 18a on 50r (R)	☐	☐	☐	☐
1913	**185**	2a on 18a on 75r (G)	☐	☐	☐	☐
1913	**186**	2a on 18a on 150r (G)	☐	☐	☐	☐
1913	**187**	½a blue green	☐	☐	☐	☐

DATE	SCOTT NO.	DESCRIPTION	UNUSED	USED		
Macao						
1913	**188**	1a red	☐	☐	☐	☐
1913	**189**	2a red violet	☐	☐	☐	☐
1913	**190**	4a yellow grn	☐	☐	☐	☐
1913	**191**	8a dk blue	☐	☐	☐	☐
1913	**192**	10a on 12a vio brn	☐	☐	☐	☐
1913	**193**	16a bister brn	☐	☐	☐	☐
1913	**194**	24a bister	☐	☐	☐	☐
1913	**195**	4a carmine (G)	☐	☐	☐	☐
1913	**196**	5a yellow brn	☐	☐	☐	☐
1913	**197**	6a red brown	☐	☐	☐	☐
1913	**198**	8a gray brown	☐	☐	☐	☐
1913	**198A**	10a dull blue	☐	☐	☐	☐
1913	**199**	13a violet	☐	☐	☐	☐
1913	**200**	13a gray lilac	☐	☐	☐	☐
1913	**201**	16a blue, bl	☐	☐	☐	☐
1913	**202**	18a org brn, pink	☐	☐	☐	☐
1913	**203**	20a brown, yelsh	☐	☐	☐	☐
1913	**204**	31a red lil, pink	☐	☐	☐	☐
1913	**205**	47a dull bl, straw	☐	☐	☐	☐
1913	**206**	½a on 5a yel brn (R)	☐	☐	☐	☐
1913	**207**	4a on 8a gray brn (R)	☐	☐	☐	☐
1913	**208**	1a on 13a violet (R)	☐	☐	☐	☐
1913	**209**	1a on 13a gray lil (R)	☐	☐	☐	☐
1913	**210**	½a olive brown	☐	☐	☐	☐
1913	**211**	1a black	☐	☐	☐	☐
1913	**212**	2a blue green	☐	☐	☐	☐
1913	**213**	4a carmine	☐	☐	☐	☐
1913	**214**	5a lilac brown	☐	☐	☐	☐
1913	**215**	6a lt violet	☐	☐	☐	☐
1913	**216**	8a lilac brown	☐	☐	☐	☐
1913	**217**	10a deep blue	☐	☐	☐	☐
1913	**218**	12a yellow brn	☐	☐	☐	☐
1913	**219**	16a slate	☐	☐	☐	☐
1913	**220**	20a orange brn	☐	☐	☐	☐
1913	**221**	40a plum	☐	☐	☐	☐
1913	**222**	58a brown, grn	☐	☐	☐	☐
1913	**223**	76a brown, pink	☐	☐	☐	☐
1913	**224**	1p orange, sal	☐	☐	☐	☐

DATE	SCOTT NO.	DESCRIPTION	UNUSED	USED		
Macao						
1913	**225**	3p green, bl	☐	☐	☐	☐
1919	**226**	½a olive brown	☐	☐	☐	☐
1919	**227**	1a black	☐	☐	☐	☐
1919	**228**	2a blue green	☐	☐	☐	☐
1919	**229**	4a carmine	☐	☐	☐	☐
1922-24	**230**	½a olive brown	☐	☐	☐	☐
1922-24	**231**	1a black	☐	☐	☐	☐
1922-24	**232**	1½a yel grn ('24)	☐	☐	☐	☐
1922-24	**233**	2a blue green	☐	☐	☐	☐
1922-24	**234**	3a org brn	☐	☐	☐	☐
1922-24	**235**	4a carmine	☐	☐	☐	☐
1922-24	**236**	4a lemon ('24)	☐	☐	☐	☐
1922-24	**237**	6a gray ('23)	☐	☐	☐	☐
1922-24	**238**	8a lilac brown	☐	☐	☐	☐
1922-24	**238A**	10a pale bl ('23)	☐	☐	☐	☐
1922-24	**238B**	12a yellow brown	☐	☐	☐	☐
1922-24	**238C**	14a lilac ('24)	☐	☐	☐	☐
1922-24	**238D**	16a slate	☐	☐	☐	☐
1922-24	**238E**	24a sl grn ('23)	☐	☐	☐	☐
1922-24	**238F**	32a org brn ('24)	☐	☐	☐	☐
1922-24	**238G**	56a dl rose ('24)	☐	☐	☐	☐
1922-24	**238H**	72a brown ('23)	☐	☐	☐	☐
1922-24	**238I**	1p org ('24)	☐	☐	☐	☐
1922-24	**238J**	3p pale turq ('24)	☐	☐	☐	☐
1922-24	**238K**	5p car rose ('24)	☐	☐	☐	☐
1915	**239**	6a on 10r green	☐	☐	☐	☐
1915	**240**	6a on 5r yellow	☐	☐	☐	☐
1915	**241**	6a on 10r red vio	☐	☐	☐	☐
1915	**242**	6a on 15r choc	☐	☐	☐	☐
1915	**243**	6a on 25r green	☐	☐	☐	☐
1915	**244**	6a on 80r yel grn	☐	☐	☐	☐
1915	**245**	6a on 100r brn, buff	☐	☐	☐	☐
1915	**246**	6a on 200r bl, bl	☐	☐	☐	☐
1915	**247**	18a on 20r lav	☐	☐	☐	☐
1915	**248**	18a on 50r lt bl	☐	☐	☐	☐
1915	**249**	18a on 75r car	☐	☐	☐	☐
1915	**250**	18a on 150r car, rose	☐	☐	☐	☐
1915	**251**	18a on 300r bl, sal	☐	☐	☐	☐

DATE	SCOTT NO.	DESCRIPTION	UNUSED	USED		
Macao						
1915	**252**	18a on 2½r brn	☐	☐	☐	☐
1915	**253**	8a blue	☐	☐	☐	☐
1915	**254**	10a slate blue	☐	☐	☐	☐
1915	**255**	10a on 12a red lil	☐	☐	☐	☐
1919-20	**256**	½a on 5a lilac brn	☐	☐	☐	☐
1919-20	**257**	2a on 6a on 25r green	☐	☐	☐	☐
1919-20	**258**	2a on 6a on 80r yel grn	☐	☐	☐	☐
1919-20	**258A**	2a on 6a red brown	☐	☐	☐	☐
1931-33	**259**	1a on 24a slate grn ('33)	☐	☐	☐	☐
1931-33	**260**	2a on 32a org brn ('33)	☐	☐	☐	☐
1931-33	**261**	4a on 12a bis brn ('33)	☐	☐	☐	☐
1931-33	**262**	5a on 6a lt gray ('33)	☐	☐	☐	☐
1931-33	**264**	7a on 8a lil brn	☐	☐	☐	☐
1931-33	**265**	12a on 14a lilac	☐	☐	☐	☐
1931-33	**266**	15a on 16a dk gray ('33)	☐	☐	☐	☐
1931-33	**267**	20a on 56a dull rose ('33)	☐	☐	☐	☐
1931-33	**263**	5a on 6a lt vio ('33)	☐	☐	☐	☐
1934, Feb. 1	**268**	½a bister	☐	☐	☐	☐
1934, Feb. 1	**269**	1a olive brown	☐	☐	☐	☐
1934, Feb. 1	**270**	2a blue green	☐	☐	☐	☐
1934, Feb. 1	**271**	3a violet	☐	☐	☐	☐
1934, Feb. 1	**272**	4a black	☐	☐	☐	☐
1934, Feb. 1	**273**	5a gray	☐	☐	☐	☐
1934, Feb. 1	**274**	6a brown	☐	☐	☐	☐
1934, Feb. 1	**275**	7a brt rose	☐	☐	☐	☐
1934, Feb. 1	**276**	8a brt blue	☐	☐	☐	☐
1934, Feb. 1	**277**	10a red orange	☐	☐	☐	☐
1934, Feb. 1	**278**	12a dark blue	☐	☐	☐	☐
1934, Feb. 1	**279**	14a olive green	☐	☐	☐	☐
1934, Feb. 1	**280**	15a maroon	☐	☐	☐	☐
1934, Feb. 1	**281**	20a orange	☐	☐	☐	☐
1934, Feb. 1	**282**	30a apple green	☐	☐	☐	☐
1934, Feb. 1	**283**	40a violet	☐	☐	☐	☐
1934, Feb. 1	**284**	50a olive bister	☐	☐	☐	☐
1934, Feb. 1	**285**	1p lt blue	☐	☐	☐	☐
1934, Feb. 1	**286**	2p brown org	☐	☐	☐	☐
1934, Feb. 1	**287**	3p emerald	☐	☐	☐	☐
1934, Feb. 1	**288**	5p dark violet	☐	☐	☐	☐

DATE	SCOTT NO.	DESCRIPTION	UNUSED	USED		
Macao						
1938, Aug. 1	**289**	1a gray green	☐	☐	☐	☐
1938, Aug. 1	**290**	2a orange brown	☐	☐	☐	☐
1938, Aug. 1	**291**	3a dk vio brn	☐	☐	☐	☐
1938, Aug. 1	**292**	4a brt green	☐	☐	☐	☐
1938, Aug. 1	**293**	5a dk carmine	☐	☐	☐	☐
1938, Aug. 1	**294**	6a slate	☐	☐	☐	☐
1938, Aug. 1	**295**	8a rose violet	☐	☐	☐	☐
1938, Aug. 1	**296**	10a brt red vio	☐	☐	☐	☐
1938, Aug. 1	**297**	12a red	☐	☐	☐	☐
1938, Aug. 1	**298**	15a orange	☐	☐	☐	☐
1938, Aug. 1	**299**	20a blue	☐	☐	☐	☐
1938, Aug. 1	**300**	40a gray black	☐	☐	☐	☐
1938, Aug. 1	**301**	50a brown	☐	☐	☐	☐
1938, Aug. 1	**302**	1p brown car	☐	☐	☐	☐
1938, Aug. 1	**303**	2p olive green	☐	☐	☐	☐
1938, Aug. 1	**304**	3p blue violet	☐	☐	☐	☐
1938, Aug. 1	**305**	5p red brown	☐	☐	☐	☐
1941	**306**	1a on 6a brown	☐	☐	☐	☐
1941	**307**	2a on 6a brown	☐	☐	☐	☐
1941	**308**	3a on 6a brown	☐	☐	☐	☐
1941	**309**	5a on 7a brt rose	☐	☐	☐	☐
1941	**310**	5a on 7a brt rose	☐	☐	☐	☐
1941	**311**	5a on 8a brt blue	☐	☐	☐	☐
1941	**312**	5a on 8a brt blue	☐	☐	☐	☐
1941	**313**	8a on 30a apple grn	☐	☐	☐	☐
1941	**314**	8a on 40a violet	☐	☐	☐	☐
1941	**315**	8a on 50a ol bis	☐	☐	☐	☐
1941	**315A**	3a on 6a slate	☐	☐	☐	☐
1942	**316**	1a olive brown	☐	☐	☐	☐
1942	**317**	2a blue green	☐	☐	☐	☐
1942	**318**	3a vio, perf. 11	☐	☐	☐	☐
1942	**319**	6a brown	☐	☐	☐	☐
1942	**320**	10a red orange	☐	☐	☐	☐
1942	**321**	20a orange	☐	☐	☐	☐
1942	**322**	30a apple green	☐	☐	☐	☐
1942	**323**	40a violet	☐	☐	☐	☐
1948, Dec. 20	**324**	1a dk brn & org	☐	☐	☐	☐
1948, Dec. 20	**325**	2a rose brn & rose	☐	☐	☐	☐

DATE	SCOTT NO.	DESCRIPTION	UNUSED	USED		
Macao						
1948, Dec. 20	**326**	3a brn vio & lil	☐	☐	☐	☐
1948, Dec. 20	**327**	8a rose car & rose	☐	☐	☐	☐
1948, Dec. 20	**328**	10a lil rose & rose	☐	☐	☐	☐
1948, Dec. 20	**329**	20a dk blue & gray	☐	☐	☐	☐
1948, Dec. 20	**330**	30a black & gray	☐	☐	☐	☐
1948, Dec. 20	**331**	50a brn & pale bis	☐	☐	☐	☐
1948, Dec. 20	**332**	1p emer & pale grn	☐	☐	☐	☐
1948, Dec. 20	**333**	2p scarlet & rose	☐	☐	☐	☐
1948, Dec. 20	**334**	3p dl grn & gray grn	☐	☐	☐	☐
1948, Dec. 20	**335**	5p vio bl & gray	☐	☐	☐	☐
1949, Feb. 1	**336**	8a scarlet	☐	☐	☐	☐
1949, Dec. 24	**337**	32a claret & rose	☐	☐	☐	☐
1950, July 26	**339**	32a dk slate gray	☐	☐	☐	☐
1950, July 26	**340**	50a carmine	☐	☐	☐	☐
1950-51	**341**	1a violet & rose	☐	☐	☐	☐
1950-51	**342**	2a ol bis & yel	☐	☐	☐	☐
1950-51	**343**	3a org red & buff	☐	☐	☐	☐
1950-51	**344**	8a slate & gray	☐	☐	☐	☐
1950-51	**345**	10a red brn & org	☐	☐	☐	☐
1950-51	**346**	30a vio bl & bl	☐	☐	☐	☐
1950-51	**347**	50a ol grn & yel grn	☐	☐	☐	☐
1950-51	**347A**	1p dk org brn & org brn	☐	☐	☐	☐
1951	**348**	1a org yel, lemon	☐	☐	☐	☐
1951	**349**	2a dk grn, blue	☐	☐	☐	☐
1951	**350**	10a vio brn, blue	☐	☐	☐	☐
1951	**351**	10a brt pink, blue	☐	☐	☐	☐
1951, Dec. 3	**352**	60a mag & pink + label	☐	☐	☐	☐
1951, Aug. 27	**353**	1a steel bl & gray bl	☐	☐	☐	☐
1951, Aug. 27	**354**	2a dk brn & ol grn	☐	☐	☐	☐
1951, Aug. 27	**355**	3a deep grn & grn	☐	☐	☐	☐
1951, Aug. 27	**356**	6a purple	☐	☐	☐	☐
1951, Aug. 27	**357**	10a red brn & org	☐	☐	☐	☐
1951, Aug. 27	**358**	20a brown car	☐	☐	☐	☐
1951, Aug. 27	**359**	30a dk brn & ol grn	☐	☐	☐	☐
1951, Aug. 27	**360**	50a red & orange	☐	☐	☐	☐
1951, Nov. 1	**361**	1p vio bl & bl	☐	☐	☐	☐
1951, Nov. 1	**362**	3p black & vio	☐	☐	☐	☐
1951, Nov. 1	**363**	5p henna brown	☐	☐	☐	☐

DATE	SCOTT NO.	DESCRIPTION	UNUSED	USED		
Macao						
1952, June 16	**364**	6a black & purple	☐	☐	☐	☐
1952, Nov. 28	**365**	3a blk, grnsh gray	☐	☐	☐	☐
1952, Nov. 28	**366**	16a choc, buff	☐	☐	☐	☐
1952, Nov. 28	**367**	40a blk, blue	☐	☐	☐	☐
1953, Apr. 28	**368**	8a choc & beige	☐	☐	☐	☐
1953, Apr. 28	**369**	10a blue blk & tan	☐	☐	☐	☐
1953, Apr. 28	**370**	50a ol grn & gray brn	☐	☐	☐	☐
1954, Mar. 9	**371**	10a multicolored	☐	☐	☐	☐
1953, Sept. 22	**372**	1a dark red	☐	☐	☐	☐
1953, Sept. 22	**373**	3a dark green	☐	☐	☐	☐
1953, Sept. 22	**374**	5a dark brown	☐	☐	☐	☐
1953, Sept. 22	**375**	10a dp grnsh blue	☐	☐	☐	☐
1953, Sept. 22	**376**	16a yellow brown	☐	☐	☐	☐
1953, Sept. 22	**377**	30a dk olive grn	☐	☐	☐	☐
1953, Sept. 22	**378**	39a violet blue	☐	☐	☐	☐
1953, Sept. 22	**379**	1p deep plum	☐	☐	☐	☐
1953, Sept. 22	**380**	3p dark gray	☐	☐	☐	☐
1953, Sept. 22	**381**	5p deep carmine	☐	☐	☐	☐
1954, Aug. 4	**382**	39a org, cream & blk	☐	☐	☐	☐
1956, May 10	**383**	1a pale green	☐	☐	☐	☐
1956, May 10	**384**	3a pale gray	☐	☐	☐	☐
1956, May 10	**385**	5a pale pink	☐	☐	☐	☐
1956, May 10	**386**	10a buff	☐	☐	☐	☐
1956, May 10	**387**	30a lt blue	☐	☐	☐	☐
1956, May 10	**388**	40a pale green	☐	☐	☐	☐
1956, May 10	**389**	90a pale gray	☐	☐	☐	☐
1956, May 10	**390**	1.50p pink	☐	☐	☐	☐
1958, Nov. 8	**391**	70a multicolored	☐	☐	☐	☐
1958, Nov. 15	**392**	20a multicolored	☐	☐	☐	☐
1960, June 25	**393**	2p multicolored	☐	☐	☐	☐
1962, Feb. 9	**394**	10a blue & yel grn	☐	☐	☐	☐
1962, Feb. 9	**395**	16a brt pink	☐	☐	☐	☐
1962, Feb. 9	**396**	20a orange	☐	☐	☐	☐
1962, Feb. 9	**397**	50a rose	☐	☐	☐	☐
1962, Feb. 9	**398**	1.20p blue & beige	☐	☐	☐	☐
1962, Feb. 9	**399**	2.50p gray & brown	☐	☐	☐	☐
1962, Apr. 7	**400**	40a multicolored	☐	☐	☐	☐
1964, May 16	**401**	20a multicolored	☐	☐	☐	☐

Macao

DATE	SCOTT NO.	DESCRIPTION	UNUSED	USED		
1965, May 17	**402**	10a pale grn & multi	☐	☐	☐	☐
1966, May 28	**403**	10a multicolored	☐	☐	☐	☐
1966, Aug. 8	**404**	10a multicolored	☐	☐	☐	☐
1966, Aug. 8	**405**	15a multicolored	☐	☐	☐	☐
1966, Aug. 8	**406**	20a multicolored	☐	☐	☐	☐
1966, Aug. 8	**407**	40a multicolored	☐	☐	☐	☐
1966, Aug. 8	**408**	50a multicolored	☐	☐	☐	☐
1966, Aug. 8	**409**	60a multicolored	☐	☐	☐	☐
1966, Aug. 8	**410**	1p multicolored	☐	☐	☐	☐
1966, Aug. 8	**411**	3p multicolored	☐	☐	☐	☐
1967, Jan. 31	**412**	10a multicolored	☐	☐	☐	☐
1967, Jan. 31	**413**	20a multicolored	☐	☐	☐	☐
1967, May 13	**414**	50a multicolored	☐	☐	☐	☐
1968, Apr. 22	**415**	20a multicolored	☐	☐	☐	☐
1968, Apr. 22	**416**	70a multicolored	☐	☐	☐	☐
1969, Feb. 17	**417**	20a multicolored	☐	☐	☐	☐
1969, Aug. 29	**418**	1p multicolored	☐	☐	☐	☐
1969, Sept. 25	**419**	90a multicolored	☐	☐	☐	☐
1969, Oct. 16	**420**	50a multicolored	☐	☐	☐	☐
1969, Dec. 1	**421**	30a multicolored	☐	☐	☐	☐
1970, Nov. 15	**422**	5a multicolored	☐	☐	☐	☐
1971, Sept. 30	**423**	5a lt blue & multi	☐	☐	☐	☐
1971, Sept. 30	**424**	10a Lion mask	☐	☐	☐	☐
1972, May 25	**425**	20a citron & multi	☐	☐	☐	☐
1972, June 20	**426**	50a multicolored	☐	☐	☐	☐
1972, Sept. 20	**427**	5p multicolored	☐	☐	☐	☐
1972, Dec. 25	**428**	2p multicolored	☐	☐	☐	☐
1973, Dec. 15	**429**	20a blue grn & multi	☐	☐	☐	☐
1974, Jan. 25	**430**	15a multicolored	☐	☐	☐	☐
1974, Jan. 25	**431**	60a multicolored	☐	☐	☐	☐
1974, Sept. 23	**432**	30a multicolored	☐	☐	☐	☐
1974, Oct. 7	**433**	20a multicolored	☐	☐	☐	☐
1974, Oct. 7	**434**	2.20p multicolored	☐	☐	☐	☐
1975, Apr. 25	**435**	10a ocher & multi	☐	☐	☐	☐
1975, Apr. 25	**436**	1p multicolored	☐	☐	☐	☐
1976, Jan. 30	**437**	10p multicolored	☐	☐	☐	☐
1976, Jan. 30	**438**	20p multicolored	☐	☐	☐	☐
1978	**440**	5a blk, dk & lt blue	☐	☐	☐	☐

DATE	SCOTT NO.	DESCRIPTION	UNUSED	USED		
Macao						
1978	**441**	2p blk, org brn & buff	☐	☐	☐	☐
1978	**442**	5p blk, ol & yel grn	☐	☐	☐	☐
1979, Nov.	**443**	10a on 16a	☐	☐	☐	☐
1979, Nov.	**444**	30a on 39a (#378)	☐	☐	☐	☐
1979, Nov.	**445**	30a on 39a (#382)	☐	☐	☐	☐
1979, Nov.	**446**	2p on 2.20p	☐	☐	☐	☐
1981, June	**447**	10a multicolored	☐	☐	☐	☐
1981, June	**448**	30a multicolored	☐	☐	☐	☐
1981, June	**449**	1p multicolored	☐	☐	☐	☐
1981, June	**450**	3p multicolored	☐	☐	☐	☐
1981, Sept.	**451**	15a multicolored	☐	☐	☐	☐
1981, Sept.	**452**	40a multicolored	☐	☐	☐	☐
1981, Sept.	**453**	50a multicolored	☐	☐	☐	☐
1981, Sept.	**454**	60a multicolored	☐	☐	☐	☐
1981, Sept.	**455**	1p multicolored	☐	☐	☐	☐
1981, Sept.	**456**	2.20p multicolored	☐	☐	☐	☐
1981	**457**	30a on 60a multi	☐	☐	☐	☐
1982, June 10	**458**	30a shown	☐	☐	☐	☐
1982, June 10	**459**	40a multicolored	☐	☐	☐	☐
1982, June 10	**460**	1p multicolored	☐	☐	☐	☐
1982, June 10	**461**	2p multicolored	☐	☐	☐	☐
1982, June 10	**462**	10p multicolored	☐	☐	☐	☐
1982, Oct. 1	**463**	40a multicolored	☐	☐	☐	☐
1982, Oct. 1	**464**	1p multicolored	☐	☐	☐	☐
1982, Oct. 1	**465**	2p multicolored	☐	☐	☐	☐
1982, Oct. 1	**466**	5p multicolored	☐	☐	☐	☐
1982, Dec. 1	**467**	50a Aerial view	☐	☐	☐	☐
1982, Dec. 1	**468**	3p Map	☐	☐	☐	☐
1983, Feb. 16	**469**	60a multicolored	☐	☐	☐	☐
1983, Feb. 16	**470**	3p multicolored	☐	☐	☐	☐
1983, Feb. 16	**471**	6p multicolored	☐	☐	☐	☐
1983, May 12	**472**	10a multi	☐	☐	☐	☐
1983, May 12	**473**	80a multi	☐	☐	☐	☐
1983, May 12	**474**	1.50p multi	☐	☐	☐	☐
1983, May 12	**475**	2.50p multi	☐	☐	☐	☐
1983, May 12	**476**	7.50p multi	☐	☐	☐	☐
1983, July 14	**477**	20a multi	☐	☐	☐	☐
1983, July 14	**478**	40a multi	☐	☐	☐	☐

DATE	SCOTT NO.	DESCRIPTION	UNUSED	USED		
Macao						
1983, July 14	**479**	60a multi	☐	☐	☐	☐
1983, July 14	**480**	70a multi	☐	☐	☐	☐
1983, July 14	**481**	1.50p multi	☐	☐	☐	☐
1983, July 14	**482**	2.50p multi	☐	☐	☐	☐
1983, Nov. 15	**483**	4p multicolored	☐	☐	☐	☐
1983, Nov. 15	**484**	4p multicolored	☐	☐	☐	☐
1984, Jan. 25	**485**	60a multicolored	☐	☐	☐	☐
1984, Mar. 1	**486**	40a orange & blk	☐	☐	☐	☐
1984, Mar. 1	**487**	3p gray & blk	☐	☐	☐	☐
1984, Mar. 1	**488**	5p sepia & blk	☐	☐	☐	☐
1984, May 18	**489**	20a multicolored	☐	☐	☐	☐
1984, May 18	**490**	60a multicolored	☐	☐	☐	☐
1984, May 18	**491**	90a multicolored	☐	☐	☐	☐
1984, May 18	**492**	3p multicolored	☐	☐	☐	☐
1984, May 18	**493**	15p multicolored	☐	☐	☐	☐
1984, Sept. 21	**494**	30a multicolored	☐	☐	☐	☐
1984, Sept. 21	**495**	40a multicolored	☐	☐	☐	☐
1984, Sept. 21	**496**	50a multicolored	☐	☐	☐	☐
1984, Sept. 21	**497**	70a multicolored	☐	☐	☐	☐
1984, Sept. 21	**498**	2.50p multicolored	☐	☐	☐	☐
1984, Sept. 21	**499**	6p multicolored	☐	☐	☐	☐
1984, Oct. 22	**500**	20a Hok lou t'eng	☐	☐	☐	☐
1984, Oct. 22	**501**	60a Tai t'ong	☐	☐	☐	☐
1984, Oct. 22	**502**	2p Tai mei chai	☐	☐	☐	☐
1984, Oct. 22	**503**	5p Ch'at pong t'o	☐	☐	☐	☐
1985, Feb. 13	**504**	1p Water buffalo	☐	☐	☐	☐
1985, Apr. 19	**505**	2.50p shown	☐	☐	☐	☐
1985, Apr. 19	**506**	3p Clasped hands	☐	☐	☐	☐
1985, May 27	**507**	1.50p multicolored	☐	☐	☐	☐
1985, June 27	**508**	2.50p multi	☐	☐	☐	☐
1985, June 27	**509**	2.50p multi	☐	☐	☐	☐
1985, June 27	**510**	2.50p multi	☐	☐	☐	☐
1985, June 27	**511**	2.50p multi	☐	☐	☐	☐
1985, Sept. 27	**512**	30a multi	☐	☐	☐	☐
1985, Sept. 27	**513**	50a multi	☐	☐	☐	☐
1985, Sept. 27	**514**	70a multi	☐	☐	☐	☐
1985, Sept. 27	**515**	2p multi	☐	☐	☐	☐
1985, Sept. 27	**516**	4p multi	☐	☐	☐	☐

DATE	SCOTT NO.	DESCRIPTION	UNUSED	USED		
Macao						
1985, Sept. 27	**517**	7.50p multi	☐	☐	☐	☐
1985, Oct. 25	**518**	50a multicolored	☐	☐	☐	☐
1985, Oct. 25	**519**	70a multicolored	☐	☐	☐	☐
1985, Oct. 25	**520**	1p multicolored	☐	☐	☐	☐
1985, Oct. 25	**521**	6p multicolored	☐	☐	☐	☐
1986, Feb. 3	**522**	1.50p Tiger	☐	☐	☐	☐
1986, Apr. 10	**523**	2.20p multicolored	☐	☐	☐	☐
1986, May 22	**524**	20a Suo-na	☐	☐	☐	☐
1986, May 22	**525**	50a Sheng	☐	☐	☐	☐
1986, May 22	**526**	60a Er-hu	☐	☐	☐	☐
1986, May 22	**527**	70a Ruan	☐	☐	☐	☐
1986, May 22	**528**	5p Cheng	☐	☐	☐	☐
1986, May 22	**529**	8p Pi-pa	☐	☐	☐	☐
1986, Aug. 28	**530**	10a Hydrofoil	☐	☐	☐	☐
1986, Aug. 28	**531**	40a Hovermarine	☐	☐	☐	☐
1986, Aug. 28	**532**	3p Jetfoil	☐	☐	☐	☐
1986, Aug. 28	**533**	7.5p High-speed ferry	☐	☐	☐	☐
1986, Oct. 3	**534**	2p multi	☐	☐	☐	☐
1986, Oct. 3	**535**	2p multi	☐	☐	☐	☐
1986, Oct. 3	**536**	2p multi	☐	☐	☐	☐
1986, Oct. 3	**537**	2p multi	☐	☐	☐	☐
1986, Nov. 12	**538**	70a multicolored	☐	☐	☐	☐
1986, Nov. 12	**539**	1.30p shown	☐	☐	☐	☐
1987, Jan. 21	**540**	1.50p Hare	☐	☐	☐	☐
1987, Apr. 10	**541**	2.20p multi	☐	☐	☐	☐
1987, Apr. 10	**542**	2.20p multi	☐	☐	☐	☐
1987, Apr. 10	**543**	2.20p multi	☐	☐	☐	☐
1987, Apr. 10	**544**	2.20p multi	☐	☐	☐	☐
1987, May 29	**545**	50a multi	☐	☐	☐	☐
1987, May 29	**546**	5p multi	☐	☐	☐	☐
1987, July 29	**547**	30a multicolored	☐	☐	☐	☐
1987, July 29	**548**	70a multi, diff.	☐	☐	☐	☐
1987, July 29	**549**	1p multi, diff.	☐	☐	☐	☐
1987, July 29	**550**	6p multi, diff.	☐	☐	☐	☐
1987, Sept. 30	**551**	20a Fan-tan	☐	☐	☐	☐
1987, Sept. 30	**552**	40a Cussec	☐	☐	☐	☐
1987, Sept. 30	**553**	4p Baccarat	☐	☐	☐	☐
1987, Sept. 30	**554**	7p Roulette	☐	☐	☐	☐

DATE	SCOTT NO.	DESCRIPTION	UNUSED	USED		
Macao						
1987, Nov. 18	**555**	10a multi	☐	☐	☐	☐
1987, Nov. 18	**556**	70a multi	☐	☐	☐	☐
1987, Nov. 18	**557**	90a multi	☐	☐	☐	☐
1987, Nov. 18	**558**	10p multi	☐	☐	☐	☐
1987, Nov. 18	**559**	7.50p Sedan chair, diff.	☐	☐	☐	☐
1988, Feb. 10	**560**	2.50p Dragon	☐	☐	☐	☐
1988, Apr. 14	**561**	3p multi	☐	☐	☐	☐
1988, Apr. 14	**562**	3p multi	☐	☐	☐	☐
1988, Apr. 14	**563**	3p multi	☐	☐	☐	☐
1988, Apr. 14	**564**	3p multi	☐	☐	☐	☐
1988, June 1	**565**	60a Breast-feeding	☐	☐	☐	☐
1988, June 1	**566**	80a Immunization	☐	☐	☐	☐
1988, June 1	**567**	2.40p Blood donation	☐	☐	☐	☐
1988, July 15	**568**	20a multi	☐	☐	☐	☐
1988, July 15	**569**	50a multi	☐	☐	☐	☐
1988, July 15	**570**	3.30p multi	☐	☐	☐	☐
1988, July 15	**571**	5p multi	☐	☐	☐	☐
1988, July 15	**572**	7.50p multi	☐	☐	☐	☐
1988, Sept. 19	**573**	40a Hurdles	☐	☐	☐	☐
1988, Sept. 19	**574**	60a Basketball	☐	☐	☐	☐
1988, Sept. 19	**575**	1p Soccer	☐	☐	☐	☐
1988, Sept. 19	**576**	8p Table tennis	☐	☐	☐	☐
1988, Sept. 19	**577**	Sheet of 5, #573-576, 577a	☐	☐	☐	☐
1988, Oct. 10	**578**	13.40p Electronic mail	☐	☐	☐	☐
1988, Oct. 10	**579**	40p Express mail	☐	☐	☐	☐
1988, Nov. 24	**580**	80a Sedan	☐	☐	☐	☐
1988, Nov. 24	**581**	2.80p Motorcycle	☐	☐	☐	☐
1988, Nov. 24	**582**	7p Formula 3	☐	☐	☐	☐
1989, Jan. 20	**583**	3p Snake	☐	☐	☐	☐
1989, Mar. 1	**584**	50a Water carrier	☐	☐	☐	☐
1989, Mar. 1	**585**	1p Tan-kya woman	☐	☐	☐	☐
1989, Mar. 1	**586**	4p Tin-tin (junk) man	☐	☐	☐	☐
1989, Mar. 1	**587**	5p Tofu peddler	☐	☐	☐	☐
1989, Apr. 10	**588**	2p multi (4-1)	☐	☐	☐	☐
1989, Apr. 10	**589**	2p multi (4-2)	☐	☐	☐	☐
1989, Apr. 10	**590**	2p multi (4-3)	☐	☐	☐	☐
1989, Apr. 10	**591**	2p multi (4-4)	☐	☐	☐	☐
1989, July 7	**592**	2.50p multicolored	☐	☐	☐	☐

DATE	SCOTT NO.	DESCRIPTION	UNUSED	USED		
Macao						
1989, July 7	**593**	2.50p multicolored	☐	☐	☐	☐
1989, July 7	**594**	2.50p multicolored	☐	☐	☐	☐
1989, July 7	**595**	2.50p multicolored	☐	☐	☐	☐
1989, July 31	**596**	10a Talu	☐	☐	☐	☐
1989, July 31	**597**	60a Triol	☐	☐	☐	☐
1989, July 31	**598**	3.30p Chiquia	☐	☐	☐	☐
1989, July 31	**599**	5p Xadrez Chines	☐	☐	☐	☐
1989, Oct. 9	**600**	50a multi	☐	☐	☐	☐
1989, Oct. 9	**601**	70a multi	☐	☐	☐	☐
1989, Oct. 9	**602**	2.80p multi	☐	☐	☐	☐
1989, Oct. 9	**603**	4p multi	☐	☐	☐	☐
1989, Oct. 9	**604**	7.50p multi	☐	☐	☐	☐
1989, Nov. 17	**605**	40a Malacca	☐	☐	☐	☐
1989, Nov. 17	**606**	70a Thailand	☐	☐	☐	☐
1989, Nov. 17	**607**	90a India	☐	☐	☐	☐
1989, Nov. 17	**608**	2.50p Japan	☐	☐	☐	☐
1989, Nov. 17	**609**	7.50p China	☐	☐	☐	☐
1989, Nov. 17	**610**	Sheet of 6, #605-609, 610a	☐	☐	☐	☐
1990, Jan. 19	**611**	4p Horse	☐	☐	☐	☐
1990, Mar. 1	**612**	30a multicolored	☐	☐	☐	☐
1990, Mar. 1	**613**	70a multicolored	☐	☐	☐	☐
1990, Mar. 1	**614**	1.50p multicolored	☐	☐	☐	☐
1990, Mar. 1	**615**	7.50p multicolored	☐	☐	☐	☐
1990, May 3	**616**	10p multicolored	☐	☐	☐	☐
1990, June 8	**617**	2.40p shown	☐	☐	☐	☐
1990, June 8	**618**	2.40p multicolored	☐	☐	☐	☐
1990, June 8	**619**	2.40p multicolored	☐	☐	☐	☐
1990, June 8	**620**	2.40p multicolored	☐	☐	☐	☐
1990, Aug. 24	**621**	3p shown	☐	☐	☐	☐
1990, Aug. 24	**622**	3p Furniture	☐	☐	☐	☐
1990, Aug. 24	**623**	3p Toys	☐	☐	☐	☐
1990, Aug. 24	**624**	3p Artificial flowers	☐	☐	☐	☐
1990, Sept. 22	**625**	80a Cycling	☐	☐	☐	☐
1990, Sept. 22	**626**	1p Swimming	☐	☐	☐	☐
1990, Sept. 22	**627**	3p Judo	☐	☐	☐	☐
1990, Sept. 22	**628**	4.20p Shooting	☐	☐	☐	☐
1990, Sept. 22	**629**	Sheet of 5, #625-628, 629a	☐	☐	☐	☐
1990, Oct. 9	**630**	50a shown	☐	☐	☐	☐

DATE	SCOTT NO.	DESCRIPTION	UNUSED	USED		
Macao						
1990, Oct. 9	**631**	1p multi, diff.	☐	☐	☐	☐
1990, Oct. 9	**632**	3.50p multi, diff.	☐	☐	☐	☐
1990, Oct. 9	**633**	6.50p multi, diff.	☐	☐	☐	☐
1990, Oct. 9	**634**	5p multi, diff.	☐	☐	☐	☐
1990, Nov. 15	**635**	20a Cricket fight	☐	☐	☐	☐
1990, Nov. 15	**636**	80a Bird fight	☐	☐	☐	☐
1990, Nov. 15	**637**	1p Greyhound race	☐	☐	☐	☐
1990, Nov. 15	**638**	10p Horse race	☐	☐	☐	☐
1991, Feb. 8	**639**	4.50p Ram	☐	☐	☐	☐
1991, Mar. 1	**640**	80a multi	☐	☐	☐	☐
1991, Mar. 1	**641**	1.70p multi	☐	☐	☐	☐
1991, Mar. 1	**642**	3.50p multi	☐	☐	☐	☐
1991, Mar. 1	**643**	4.20p multi	☐	☐	☐	☐
1991, Apr. 18	**644**	3p multi	☐	☐	☐	☐
1991, Apr. 18	**645**	3p multi	☐	☐	☐	☐
1991, Apr. 18	**646**	3p multi	☐	☐	☐	☐
1991, Apr. 18	**647**	3p multi	☐	☐	☐	☐
1991, June 5	**648**	60a multicolored	☐	☐	☐	☐
1991, June 5	**649**	80a multicolored	☐	☐	☐	☐
1991, June 5	**650**	1p multicolored	☐	☐	☐	☐
1991, June 5	**651**	10p multicolored	☐	☐	☐	☐
1991, Oct. 9	**652**	1.70p multicolored	☐	☐	☐	☐
1991, Oct. 9	**653**	3p multicolored	☐	☐	☐	☐
1991, Oct. 9	**654**	3.50p multicolored	☐	☐	☐	☐
1991, Oct. 9	**655**	4.20p multicolored	☐	☐	☐	☐
1991, Nov. 16	**656**	4.20p multicolored	☐	☐	☐	☐
1991, Nov. 16	**657**	4.20p shown	☐	☐	☐	☐
1991, Nov. 29	**658**	1.70p multicolored	☐	☐	☐	☐
1991, Nov. 29	**659**	3p multicolored	☐	☐	☐	☐
1991, Nov. 29	**660**	3.50p multicolored	☐	☐	☐	☐
1991, Nov. 29	**661**	4.20p multicolored	☐	☐	☐	☐
1992, Jan. 28	**662**	4.50p Monkey	☐	☐	☐	☐
1992, Mar. 1	**663**	1.70p multicolored	☐	☐	☐	☐
1992, Mar. 1	**664**	3p multi, diff.	☐	☐	☐	☐
1992, Mar. 1	**665**	3.50p multi, diff.	☐	☐	☐	☐
1992, Mar. 1	**666**	4.20p multi, diff.	☐	☐	☐	☐
1992, Apr. 3	**667**	3.50p multi	☐	☐	☐	☐
1992, Apr. 3	**668**	3.50p multi	☐	☐	☐	☐

DATE	SCOTT NO.	DESCRIPTION	UNUSED	USED		
Macao						
1992, Apr. 3	**669**	3.50p multi	☐	☐	☐	☐
1992, Apr. 3	**670**	3.50p multi	☐	☐	☐	☐
1992, May 18	**671**	1p multicolored	☐	☐	☐	☐
1992, May 18	**672**	2.70p multicolored	☐	☐	☐	☐
1992, May 18	**673**	6p multicolored	☐	☐	☐	☐
1992, July 1	**674**	80a High jump	☐	☐	☐	☐
1992, July 1	**675**	4.20p Badminton	☐	☐	☐	☐
1992, July 1	**676**	4.70p Roller hockey	☐	☐	☐	☐
1992, July 1	**677**	5p Yachting	☐	☐	☐	☐
1992, Oct. 9	**678**	1p Na Cha	☐	☐	☐	☐
1992, Oct. 9	**679**	1.50p Kun Iam	☐	☐	☐	☐
1992, Oct. 9	**680**	1.70p Hong Kon	☐	☐	☐	☐
1992, Oct. 9	**681**	6.50p A Ma	☐	☐	☐	☐
1992, Nov. 1	**682**	10p multicolored	☐	☐	☐	☐
1992, Nov. 27	**683**	1p multicolored	☐	☐	☐	☐
1993, Jan. 18	**684**	5p Rooster	☐	☐	☐	☐
1993, Mar. 1	**685**	50a T'am Kong	☐	☐	☐	☐
1993, Mar. 1	**686**	2p T'in Hau	☐	☐	☐	☐
1993, Mar. 1	**687**	3.50p Lin Fong	☐	☐	☐	☐
1993, Mar. 1	**688**	8p Pau Kong	☐	☐	☐	☐
1993, Apr. 1	**689**	3.50p multi (4-1)	☐	☐	☐	☐
1993, Apr. 1	**690**	3.50p multi (4-2)	☐	☐	☐	☐
1993, Apr. 1	**691**	3.50p multi (4-3)	☐	☐	☐	☐
1993, Apr. 1	**692**	3.50p multi (4-4)	☐	☐	☐	☐
1993, May 19	**693**	3p multicolored	☐	☐	☐	☐
1993, May 19	**694**	3p multicolored	☐	☐	☐	☐
1993, May 19	**695**	3p multicolored	☐	☐	☐	☐
1993, May 19	**696**	3p multicolored	☐	☐	☐	☐
1993, May 19	**697**	8p multicolored	☐	☐	☐	☐
1993, June 5	**698**	1p multicolored	☐	☐	☐	☐
1993, June 27	**699**	3p multicolored	☐	☐	☐	☐
1993, June 27	**700**	3p multicolored	☐	☐	☐	☐
1993, June 27	**701**	3p multicolored	☐	☐	☐	☐
1993, June 27	**702**	3p multicolored	☐	☐	☐	☐
1993, July 30	**703**	1.50p multicolored	☐	☐	☐	☐
1993, Sept. 22	**704**	50a multicolored	☐	☐	☐	☐
1993, Sept. 22	**705**	3p multicolored	☐	☐	☐	☐
1993, Sept. 22	**706**	3.50p multicolored	☐	☐	☐	☐

DATE	SCOTT NO.	DESCRIPTION	UNUSED	USED		
Macao						
1993, Oct. 9	**707**	1p multicolored	☐	☐	☐	☐
1993, Oct. 9	**708**	2p multicolored	☐	☐	☐	☐
1993, Oct. 9	**709**	3p multicolored	☐	☐	☐	☐
1993, Oct. 9	**710**	8p multicolored	☐	☐	☐	☐
1993, Nov. 5	**711**	1p Caravel	☐	☐	☐	☐
1993, Nov. 5	**712**	2p Round caravel	☐	☐	☐	☐
1993, Nov. 5	**713**	3.50p Nau	☐	☐	☐	☐
1993, Nov. 5	**714**	4.50p Galleon	☐	☐	☐	☐
1993, Nov. 16	**715**	1.50p Stock car	☐	☐	☐	☐
1993, Nov. 16	**716**	2p Motorcycle	☐	☐	☐	☐
1993, Nov. 16	**717**	4.50p Formula 1 race car	☐	☐	☐	☐
1994, Feb. 3	**718**	5p Dog	☐	☐	☐	☐
1994, Mar. 4	**719**	3p multicolored	☐	☐	☐	☐
1994, Mar. 21	**720**	3.50p multi (4-1)	☐	☐	☐	☐
1994, Mar. 21	**721**	3.50p multi (4-2)	☐	☐	☐	☐
1994, Mar. 21	**722**	3.50p multi (4-3)	☐	☐	☐	☐
1994, Mar. 21	**723**	3.50p multi (4-4)	☐	☐	☐	☐
1994, Apr. 6	**724**	1p multicolored	☐	☐	☐	☐
1994, Apr. 6	**725**	2p multicolored	☐	☐	☐	☐
1994, Apr. 6	**726**	3.50p multicolored	☐	☐	☐	☐
1994, Apr. 6	**727**	4.50p multicolored	☐	☐	☐	☐
1994, May 9	**728**	3p multi (3-1)	☐	☐	☐	☐
1994, May 9	**729**	3p multi (3-2)	☐	☐	☐	☐
1994, May 9	**730**	3p multi (3-3)	☐	☐	☐	☐
1994, June 1	**731**	2p multicolored	☐	☐	☐	☐
1994, June 1	**732**	3p multicolored	☐	☐	☐	☐
1994, June 1	**733**	3.50p multicolored	☐	☐	☐	☐
1994, June 1	**734**	4.50p multicolored	☐	☐	☐	☐
1994, June 27	**735**	1p multi	☐	☐	☐	☐
1994, June 27	**736**	1.50p multi	☐	☐	☐	☐
1994, June 27	**737**	2p multi	☐	☐	☐	☐
1994, June 27	**738**	3.50p multi	☐	☐	☐	☐
1994, Sept. 13	**739**	3p Astrolabe	☐	☐	☐	☐
1994, Sept. 13	**740**	3.50p Quadrant	☐	☐	☐	☐
1994, Sept. 13	**741**	4.50p Sextant	☐	☐	☐	☐
1994, Sept. 30	**742**	1p Fencing	☐	☐	☐	☐
1994, Sept. 30	**743**	2p Gymnastics	☐	☐	☐	☐
1994, Sept. 30	**744**	3p Water polo	☐	☐	☐	☐

DATE	SCOTT NO.	DESCRIPTION	UNUSED	USED		
Macao						
1994, Sept. 30	**745**	3.50p Pole vault	☐	☐	☐	☐
1994, Oct. 8	**746**	1p Nobre de Carvalho	☐	☐	☐	☐
1994, Oct. 8	**747**	8p Friendship	☐	☐	☐	☐
1994, Nov. 7	**748**	3p multicolored	☐	☐	☐	☐
1994, Nov. 7	**749**	3.50p multicolored	☐	☐	☐	☐
1994, Nov. 7	**750**	4.50p multicolored	☐	☐	☐	☐
1994, Nov. 30	**751**	50a multicolored	☐	☐	☐	☐
1994, Nov. 30	**752**	1p multicolored	☐	☐	☐	☐
1994, Nov. 30	**753**	1.50p multicolored	☐	☐	☐	☐
1994, Nov. 30	**754**	2p multicolored	☐	☐	☐	☐
1994, Nov. 30	**755**	3p multicolored	☐	☐	☐	☐
1994, Nov. 30	**756**	3.50p multicolored	☐	☐	☐	☐
1995, Jan. 23	**757**	5.50p Boar	☐	☐	☐	☐
1995, Mar. 1	**758**	50a multicolored	☐	☐	☐	☐
1995, Mar. 1	**759**	1p multicolored	☐	☐	☐	☐
1995, Mar. 1	**760**	1.50p multicolored	☐	☐	☐	☐
1995, Mar. 1	**761**	2p multicolored	☐	☐	☐	☐
1995, Mar. 1	**762**	2.50p multicolored	☐	☐	☐	☐
1995, Mar. 1	**763**	3p multicolored	☐	☐	☐	☐
1995, Mar. 1	**764**	3.50p multicolored	☐	☐	☐	☐
1995, Mar. 1	**765**	4p multicolored	☐	☐	☐	☐
1995, Mar. 15	**766**	1p multicolored	☐	☐	☐	☐
1995, Apr. 10	**767**	1.50p multi	☐	☐	☐	☐
1995, Apr. 10	**768**	1.50p multi	☐	☐	☐	☐
1995, Apr. 10	**769**	1.50p multi	☐	☐	☐	☐
1995, Apr. 10	**770**	1.50p multi	☐	☐	☐	☐
1995, May 5	**771**	3p multicolored	☐	☐	☐	☐
1995, May 5	**772**	3p multicolored	☐	☐	☐	☐
1995, May 5	**773**	3p multicolored	☐	☐	☐	☐
1995, May 5	**774**	3p multicolored	☐	☐	☐	☐
1995, May 5	**775**	8p multicolored	☐	☐	☐	☐
1995, June 24	**776**	2p multicolored	☐	☐	☐	☐
1995, June 24	**777**	2p multicolored	☐	☐	☐	☐
1995, June 24	**778**	2p multicolored	☐	☐	☐	☐
1995, June 24	**779**	2p multicolored	☐	☐	☐	☐
1995, June 24	**780**	8p multicolored	☐	☐	☐	☐
1995, July 17	**781**	50a Kuan Tai	☐	☐	☐	☐
1995, July 17	**782**	1p Pak Tai	☐	☐	☐	☐

DATE	SCOTT NO.	DESCRIPTION	UNUSED	USED		
Macao						
1995, July 17	**783**	1.50p Lin K'ai	☐	☐	☐	☐
1995, July 17	**784**	3p Sek Kam Tong	☐	☐	☐	☐
1995, July 17	**785**	3.50p Fok Tak	☐	☐	☐	☐
1995, Sept. 1	**786**	2.50p multicolored	☐	☐	☐	☐
1995, Sept. 1	**787**	2.50p multicolored	☐	☐	☐	☐
1995, Sept. 1	**788**	2.50p multicolored	☐	☐	☐	☐
1995, Sept. 1	**789**	2.50p multicolored	☐	☐	☐	☐
1995, Sept. 1	**790**	10p multicolored	☐	☐	☐	☐
1995, Oct. 9	**791**	1p Pipa (6-1)	☐	☐	☐	☐
1995, Oct. 9	**792**	1p Erhu (6-2)	☐	☐	☐	☐
1995, Oct. 9	**793**	1p Gongo (6-3)	☐	☐	☐	☐
1995, Oct. 9	**794**	1p Sheng (6-4)	☐	☐	☐	☐
1995, Oct. 9	**795**	1p Xiao (6-5)	☐	☐	☐	☐
1995, Oct. 9	**796**	1p Tambor (6-6)	☐	☐	☐	☐
1995, Oct. 9	**797**	8p Musicians, horiz.	☐	☐	☐	☐
1995, Oct. 24	**798**	4.50p multicolored	☐	☐	☐	☐
1995, Dec. 8	**799**	1p multicolored	☐	☐	☐	☐
1995, Dec. 8	**800**	1.50p multicolored	☐	☐	☐	☐
1995, Dec. 8	**801**	2p multicolored	☐	☐	☐	☐
1995, Dec. 8	**802**	3p multicolored	☐	☐	☐	☐
1995, Dec. 8	**803**	8p multicolored	☐	☐	☐	☐
1995, Dec. 15	**804**	1.50p #a.-l. + label	☐	☐	☐	☐
1996, Feb. 12	**805**	5p multicolored	☐	☐	☐	☐
1996, Feb. 12	**806**	10p like No. 805	☐	☐	☐	☐
1996, Mar. 1	**807**	1p multi (4-1)	☐	☐	☐	☐
1996, Mar. 1	**808**	1.50p multi (4-2)	☐	☐	☐	☐
1996, Mar. 1	**809**	3p multi (4-3)	☐	☐	☐	☐
1996, Mar. 1	**810**	4.50p multi (4-4)	☐	☐	☐	☐
1996, Mar. 1	**811**	10p purple & multi	☐	☐	☐	☐
1996, Apr. 1	**812**	50a multi (4-1)	☐	☐	☐	☐
1996, Apr. 1	**813**	1.50p multi (4-2)	☐	☐	☐	☐
1996, Apr. 1	**814**	3p multi (4-3)	☐	☐	☐	☐
1996, Apr. 1	**815**	5p multi (4-4)	☐	☐	☐	☐
1996, Apr. 1	**816**	10p multi	☐	☐	☐	☐
1996, Apr. 30	**817**	3.50p multi	☐	☐	☐	☐
1996, Apr. 30	**818**	3.50p multi	☐	☐	☐	☐
1996, Apr. 30	**819**	3.50p multi	☐	☐	☐	☐
1996, May 17	**820**	2p multi (4-1)	☐	☐	☐	☐

DATE	SCOTT NO.	DESCRIPTION	UNUSED	USED		
Macao						
1996, May 17	**821**	2p multi (4-2)	☐	☐	☐	☐
1996, May 17	**822**	2p multi (4-3)	☐	☐	☐	☐
1996, May 17	**823**	2p multi (4-4)	☐	☐	☐	☐
1996, May 17	**824**	8p multi	☐	☐	☐	☐
1996, June 14	**825**	50a multi (4-1)	☐	☐	☐	☐
1996, June 14	**826**	1.50p multi (4-2)	☐	☐	☐	☐
1996, June 14	**827**	3p multi (4-3)	☐	☐	☐	☐
1996, June 14	**828**	4p multi (4-4)	☐	☐	☐	☐
1996, July 19	**829**	2p multi	☐	☐	☐	☐
1996, July 19	**830**	3p multi	☐	☐	☐	☐
1996, July 19	**831**	3.50p multi	☐	☐	☐	☐
1996, July 19	**832**	4.50p multi	☐	☐	☐	☐
1996, July 19	**833**	10p multi	☐	☐	☐	☐
1996, Sept. 18	**834**	2.50p bl & multi (4-1)	☐	☐	☐	☐
1996, Sept. 18	**835**	2.50p grn & multi (4-2)	☐	☐	☐	☐
1996, Sept. 18	**836**	2.50p grn & multi (4-3)	☐	☐	☐	☐
1996, Sept. 18	**837**	2.50p pur & multi (4-4)	☐	☐	☐	☐
1996, Oct. 9	**838**	3p multi (4-1)	☐	☐	☐	☐
1996, Oct. 9	**839**	3p multi (4-2)	☐	☐	☐	☐
1996, Oct. 9	**840**	3p multi (4-3)	☐	☐	☐	☐
1996, Oct. 9	**841**	3p multi (4-4)	☐	☐	☐	☐
1996, Oct. 15	**842**	2.80p multicolored	☐	☐	☐	☐
1996, Oct. 15	**843**	8p like No. 842	☐	☐	☐	☐
1996, Oct. 21	**844**	3.50p multi	☐	☐	☐	☐
1996, Oct. 21	**845**	3.50p multi	☐	☐	☐	☐
1996, Oct. 21	**846**	3.50p multi	☐	☐	☐	☐
1996, Oct. 21	**847**	3.50p multi	☐	☐	☐	☐
1996, Oct. 21	**848**	8p multi	☐	☐	☐	☐
1996, Nov. 13	**849**	50a shown	☐	☐	☐	☐
1996, Nov. 13	**850**	1p Fish	☐	☐	☐	☐
1996, Nov. 13	**851**	3p Doll	☐	☐	☐	☐
1996, Nov. 13	**852**	4.50p Dragon	☐	☐	☐	☐
1997, Jan. 23	**853**	5.50p multicolored	☐	☐	☐	☐
1997, Jan. 23	**854**	10p multicolored	☐	☐	☐	☐
1997, Feb. 12	**855**	2p multi	☐	☐	☐	☐
1997, Feb. 12	**856**	2.80p multi	☐	☐	☐	☐
1997, Feb. 12	**857**	3p multi	☐	☐	☐	☐
1997, Feb. 12	**858**	3.90p multi	☐	☐	☐	☐

DATE	SCOTT NO.	DESCRIPTION	UNUSED	USED		
Macao						
1997, Feb. 12	**859**	9p multi	☐	☐	☐	☐
1997, Mar. 1	**860**	2p multicolored	☐	☐	☐	☐
1997, Mar. 1	**861**	3p multicolored	☐	☐	☐	☐
1997, Mar. 1	**862**	3.50p multicolored	☐	☐	☐	☐
1997, Mar. 1	**863**	4.50p multicolored	☐	☐	☐	☐
1997, Mar. 1	**864**	8p multicolored	☐	☐	☐	☐
1997, Mar. 26	**865**	1p multicolored	☐	☐	☐	☐
1997, Mar. 26	**866**	1.50p multicolored	☐	☐	☐	☐
1997, Mar. 26	**867**	2.50p multicolored	☐	☐	☐	☐
1997, Mar. 26	**868**	5.50p multicolored	☐	☐	☐	☐
1997, Apr. 29	**869**	3.50p multicolored	☐	☐	☐	☐
1997, Apr. 29	**870**	3.50p multicolored	☐	☐	☐	☐
1997, Apr. 29	**871**	3.50p multicolored	☐	☐	☐	☐
1997, Apr. 29	**872**	3.50p multicolored	☐	☐	☐	☐
1997, Apr. 29	**873**	8p multicolored	☐	☐	☐	☐
1997, May 14	**874**	2p multicolored	☐	☐	☐	☐
1997, May 14	**875**	3p multicolored	☐	☐	☐	☐
1997, May 14	**876**	5p multicolored	☐	☐	☐	☐
1997, May 14	**877**	9p multicolored	☐	☐	☐	☐
1997, June 9	**878**	2.50p multi (2-1)	☐	☐	☐	☐
1997, June 9	**879**	2.50p multi (2-2)	☐	☐	☐	☐
1997, June 18	**880**	2.50p multicolored	☐	☐	☐	☐
1997, June 18	**881**	2.50p multicolored	☐	☐	☐	☐
1997, June 18	**882**	2.50p multicolored	☐	☐	☐	☐
1997, June 18	**883**	2.50p multicolored	☐	☐	☐	☐
1997, June 18	**884**	10p multicolored	☐	☐	☐	☐
1997, July 12	**885**	1.50p multicolored	☐	☐	☐	☐
1997, July 30	**886**	50a multi (6-1)	☐	☐	☐	☐
1997, July 30	**887**	1p multi (6-2)	☐	☐	☐	☐
1997, July 30	**888**	1.50p multi (6-3)	☐	☐	☐	☐
1997, July 30	**889**	2p multi (6-4)	☐	☐	☐	☐
1997, July 30	**890**	2.50p multi (6-5)	☐	☐	☐	☐
1997, July 30	**891**	3p multi (6-6)	☐	☐	☐	☐
1997, July 30	**892**	8p multicolored	☐	☐	☐	☐
1997, Sept. 24	**893**	50a Planta (4-1)	☐	☐	☐	☐
1997, Sept. 24	**894**	1p Papel (4-2)	☐	☐	☐	☐
1997, Sept. 24	**895**	3.50p Seda (4-3)	☐	☐	☐	☐
1997, Sept. 24	**896**	4p Pluma (4-4)	☐	☐	☐	☐

DATE	SCOTT NO.	DESCRIPTION	UNUSED	USED		
Macao						
1997, Sept. 24	**897**	9p Sandalo	☐	☐	☐	☐
1997, Oct. 9	**898**	50a green & multi	☐	☐	☐	☐
1997, Oct. 9	**899**	1p orange & multi	☐	☐	☐	☐
1997, Oct. 9	**900**	1.50p brown & multi	☐	☐	☐	☐
1997, Oct. 9	**901**	2p yellow & multi	☐	☐	☐	☐
1997, Oct. 9	**902**	2.50p blue & multi	☐	☐	☐	☐
1997, Oct. 9	**903**	10p green & multi	☐	☐	☐	☐
1997, Nov. 19	**904**	1.50p Kung Fu	☐	☐	☐	☐
1997, Nov. 19	**905**	3.50p Judo	☐	☐	☐	☐
1997, Nov. 19	**906**	4p Karate	☐	☐	☐	☐
1998, Jan. 18	**907**	5.50p multicolored	☐	☐	☐	☐
1998, Jan. 18	**908**	10p multicolored	☐	☐	☐	☐
1998, Feb. 13	**909**	1p multi (6-1)	☐	☐	☐	☐
1998, Feb. 13	**910**	1.50p multi (6-2)	☐	☐	☐	☐
1998, Feb. 13	**911**	2p multi (6-3)	☐	☐	☐	☐
1998, Feb. 13	**912**	2.50p multi (6-4)	☐	☐	☐	☐
1998, Feb. 13	**913**	3p multi (6-5)	☐	☐	☐	☐
1998, Feb. 13	**914**	3.50p multi (6-6)	☐	☐	☐	☐
1998, Feb. 13	**915**	6p multicolored	☐	☐	☐	☐
1998, Mar. 1	**916**	50a multi (4-1)	☐	☐	☐	☐
1998, Mar. 1	**917**	1p multi (4-2)	☐	☐	☐	☐
1998, Mar. 1	**918**	3.50p multi (4-3)	☐	☐	☐	☐
1998, Mar. 1	**919**	4p multi (4-4)	☐	☐	☐	☐
1998, Mar. 1	**920**	9p multicolored	☐	☐	☐	☐
1998, Apr. 23	**921**	4p multi (4-1)	☐	☐	☐	☐
1998, Apr. 23	**922**	4p multi (4-2)	☐	☐	☐	☐
1998, Apr. 23	**923**	4p multi (4-3)	☐	☐	☐	☐
1998, Apr. 23	**924**	4p multi (4-4)	☐	☐	☐	☐
1998, Apr. 23	**925**	10p multicolored	☐	☐	☐	☐
1998, May 20	**926**	1p multi (3-1)	☐	☐	☐	☐
1998, May 20	**927**	1.50p multi (3-2)	☐	☐	☐	☐
1998, May 20	**928**	2p multi (3-3)	☐	☐	☐	☐
1998, May 20	**929**	8p multicolored	☐	☐	☐	☐
1998, May 22	**930**	2.50p multi (2-1)	☐	☐	☐	☐
1998, May 22	**931**	3p multi (2-2)	☐	☐	☐	☐
1998, May 22	**932**	9p multicolored	☐	☐	☐	☐
1998, June 10	**933**	3p multicolored	☐	☐	☐	☐
1998, June 10	**934**	3.50p multicolored	☐	☐	☐	☐

DATE	SCOTT NO.	DESCRIPTION	UNUSED	USED		
Macao						
1998, June 10	**935**	4p multicolored	☐	☐	☐	☐
1998, June 10	**936**	4.50p multicolored	☐	☐	☐	☐
1998, June 10	**937**	9p multicolored	☐	☐	☐	☐
1998, July 28	**938**	1.50p multi	☐	☐	☐	☐
1998, July 28	**939**	2p multi	☐	☐	☐	☐
1998, July 28	**940**	3p multi	☐	☐	☐	☐
1998, July 28	**941**	5p multi	☐	☐	☐	☐
1998, July 28	**942**	8p multi	☐	☐	☐	☐
1998, Sept. 4	**943**	1p like #926	☐	☐	☐	☐
1998, Sept. 4	**944**	1.50p like #927	☐	☐	☐	☐
1998, Sept. 4	**945**	2p like #928	☐	☐	☐	☐
1998, Sept. 4	**946**	8p like #929	☐	☐	☐	☐
1998, Sept. 9	**947**	50a multi (4-1)	☐	☐	☐	☐
1998, Sept. 9	**948**	1p multi (4-2)	☐	☐	☐	☐
1998, Sept. 9	**949**	1.50p multi (4-3)	☐	☐	☐	☐
1998, Sept. 9	**950**	2p multi (4-4)	☐	☐	☐	☐
1998, Sept. 9	**951**	9p multicolored	☐	☐	☐	☐
1998	**952**	3.50p multicolored	☐	☐	☐	☐
1998	**953**	3.50p multicolored	☐	☐	☐	☐
1998	**954**	3.50p multicolored	☐	☐	☐	☐
1998	**955**	3.50p multicolored	☐	☐	☐	☐
1998	**956**	10p multicolored	☐	☐	☐	☐
1998, Nov. 11	**957**	2p multi (4-1)	☐	☐	☐	☐
1998, Nov. 11	**958**	3p multi (4-2)	☐	☐	☐	☐
1998, Nov. 11	**959**	3.50p multi (4-3)	☐	☐	☐	☐
1998, Nov. 11	**960**	4.50p multi (4-4)	☐	☐	☐	☐
1998, Nov. 11	**961**	8p multicolored	☐	☐	☐	☐
1998, Dec. 8	**962**	1p multi (4-1)	☐	☐	☐	☐
1998, Dec. 8	**963**	1.50p multi (4-2)	☐	☐	☐	☐
1998, Dec. 8	**964**	2.50p multi (4-3)	☐	☐	☐	☐
1998, Dec. 8	**965**	5.50p multi (4-4)	☐	☐	☐	☐
1998, Dec. 8	**966**	10p multicolored	☐	☐	☐	☐
1999, Feb. 8	**967**	5.50p multicolored	☐	☐	☐	☐
1999, Feb. 8	**968**	10p multicolored	☐	☐	☐	☐
1999, Mar. 1	**969**	2p Bao Yu (6-1)	☐	☐	☐	☐
1999, Mar. 1	**970**	2p Dayiu (6-2)	☐	☐	☐	☐
1999, Mar. 1	**971**	2p Bao Chai (6-3)	☐	☐	☐	☐
1999, Mar. 1	**972**	2p Xi Feng (6-4)	☐	☐	☐	☐

DATE	SCOTT NO.	DESCRIPTION	UNUSED	USED		
Macao						
1999, Mar. 1	**973**	2p San Jie (6-5)	☐	☐	☐	☐
1999, Mar. 1	**974**	2p Qing Wen (6-6)	☐	☐	☐	☐
1999, Mar. 1	**975**	8p Bao Yu & Dayiu	☐	☐	☐	☐
1999, Mar. 19	**976**	1.50p Sailing ships	☐	☐	☐	☐
1999, Mar. 19	**977**	2.50p Marine life	☐	☐	☐	☐
1999, Mar. 19	**978**	6p Whale, vert.	☐	☐	☐	☐
1999, Apr. 19	**979**	3p multicolored	☐	☐	☐	☐
1999, Apr. 19	**980**	3p multicolored	☐	☐	☐	☐
1999, Apr. 28	**981**	#a.-d.	☐	☐	☐	☐
1999, Apr. 28	**982**	7p multicolored	☐	☐	☐	☐
1999, May 5	**983**	Strip of 5, #a.-e.	☐	☐	☐	☐
1999, May 5	**984**	8p multi	☐	☐	☐	☐
1999, June 2	**989**	1p multi	☐	☐	☐	☐
1999, June 2	**990**	1.50p multi	☐	☐	☐	☐
1999, June 2	**991**	2p multi	☐	☐	☐	☐
1999, June 2	**992**	2.50p multi	☐	☐	☐	☐
1999, June 2	**993**	3p multi	☐	☐	☐	☐
1999, June 2	**994**	3.50p multi, vert.	☐	☐	☐	☐
1999, June 2	**995**	4.50p multi, vert.	☐	☐	☐	☐
1999, June 2	**996**	5p multi, vert.	☐	☐	☐	☐
1999, June 2	**997**	8p multi, vert.	☐	☐	☐	☐
1999, June 2	**998**	12p multi, vert.	☐	☐	☐	☐
1999, June 24	**999**	1.50p Strip of 4, #a.-d.	☐	☐	☐	☐
1999, June 24	**1000**	10p multicolored	☐	☐	☐	☐
1999, Aug. 21	**1001**	2.50p Strip of 4, #a.-d.	☐	☐	☐	☐
1999, Aug. 21	**1002**	9p multicolored	☐	☐	☐	☐
1999, Oct. 9	**1003**	1p red violet	☐	☐	☐	☐
1999, Oct. 9	**1004**	1.50p brown, vert.	☐	☐	☐	☐
1999, Oct. 9	**1005**	2.50p gray brn, vert.	☐	☐	☐	☐
1999, Oct. 9	**1006**	3.50p blue grn	☐	☐	☐	☐
1999, Oct. 9	**1007**	10p blue gray	☐	☐	☐	☐
1999, Nov. 19	**1008**	Strip of 4, #a.-d.	☐	☐	☐	☐
1999, Nov. 19	**1009**	10p multi	☐	☐	☐	☐
1999, Dec. 19	**1010**	Block or strip of 4, #a.-d.	☐	☐	☐	☐
1999, Dec. 19	**1011**	9p multi	☐	☐	☐	☐
1999, Dec. 20	**1012**	Block of 6, #a.-f.	☐	☐	☐	☐
1999, Dec. 20	**1013**	8p multi	☐	☐	☐	☐
2000, Jan. 1	**1014**	8p multi	☐	☐	☐	☐

DATE	SCOTT NO.	DESCRIPTION	UNUSED	USED		
Macao						
2000, Jan. 28	**1015**	5.50p multi	☐	☐	☐	☐
2000, Jan. 28	**1016**	10p multi	☐	☐	☐	☐
2000, Mar. 1	**1017**	Strip of 4	☐	☐	☐	☐
2000, Mar. 1	**1018**	9p Brown circles	☐	☐	☐	☐
2000, Mar. 23	**1019**	Block of 4	☐	☐	☐	☐
2000, Mar. 23	**1020**	8p multi	☐	☐	☐	☐
2000, May 5	**1021**	Block of 6, #a-f	☐	☐	☐	☐
2000, May 5	**1022**	9p multi	☐	☐	☐	☐
2000, June 8	**1023-1026**	Set of 4	☐	☐	☐	☐
2000, June 8	**1027**	9p Chinese checkers	☐	☐	☐	☐
2000, July 7	**1028**	Horiz. strip of 4	☐	☐	☐	☐
2000, July 7	**1029**	8p Woman pouring tea	☐	☐	☐	☐
2000, Sept. 1	**1030**	2p Block of 6, #a-f	☐	☐	☐	☐
2000, Sept. 1	**1031**	8p multi	☐	☐	☐	☐
2000, Oct. 9	**1032-1035**	Set of 4	☐	☐	☐	☐
2000, Oct. 9	**1036**	10p multi	☐	☐	☐	☐
2000, Oct. 31	**1037**	2.50p Sheet of 6, #a-f	☐	☐	☐	☐
2000, Oct. 31	**1038**	8p Plate design	☐	☐	☐	☐
2000, Nov. 22	**1039-1042**	Set of 4	☐	☐	☐	☐
2000, Nov. 22	**1043**	9p multi	☐	☐	☐	☐
2000, Dec. 20	**1044**	Horiz. pair, #a-b	☐	☐	☐	☐
2000, Dec. 20	**1045**	18p Flags, monument	☐	☐	☐	☐
2001, Jan. 18	**1046**	5.50p multi	☐	☐	☐	☐
2001, Jan. 18	**1047**	10p multi	☐	☐	☐	☐
2001, Feb. 1	**1048**	2p multi	☐	☐	☐	☐
2001, Feb. 1	**1049**	2p multi	☐	☐	☐	☐
2001, Feb. 1	**1050**	2p multi	☐	☐	☐	☐
2001, Feb. 1	**1051**	2p multi	☐	☐	☐	☐
2001, Feb. 1	**1052**	8p multi	☐	☐	☐	☐
2001, Mar. 1	**1053-1056**	Set of 4	☐	☐	☐	☐
2001, Mar. 1	**1057**	8p multi	☐	☐	☐	☐
2001, Apr. 12	**1058**	Strip or block of 4	☐	☐	☐	☐
2001, Apr. 12	**1059**	8p multi	☐	☐	☐	☐
2001, May 2	**1060**	Horiz. strip of 4	☐	☐	☐	☐
2001, May 2	**1061**	8p multi	☐	☐	☐	☐
2001, June 30	**1062-1065**	Set of 4	☐	☐	☐	☐
2001, June 30	**1066**	6p multi	☐	☐	☐	☐
2001, July 14	**1067**	1p multi + label	☐	☐	☐	☐

Macao

DATE	SCOTT NO.	DESCRIPTION	UNUSED	USED		
2001, Aug. 1	**1068**	3p Block of 4, #a-d	☐	☐	☐	☐
2001, Aug. 1	**1069**	7p multi	☐	☐	☐	☐
2001, Aug. 23	**1070-1072**	Set of 3	☐	☐	☐	☐
2001, Aug. 23	**1073**	6p multi	☐	☐	☐	☐
2001, Sept. 13	**1074**	Block of 4, #a-d	☐	☐	☐	☐
2001, Sept. 13	**1075**	7p multi	☐	☐	☐	☐
2001, Oct. 9	**1076**	Block of 4, #a-d	☐	☐	☐	☐
2001, Oct. 9	**1077**	8p multi	☐	☐	☐	☐
2001, Nov. 30	**1078**	Block of 4, #a-d	☐	☐	☐	☐
2001, Nov. 30	**1079**	8p multi	☐	☐	☐	☐
2001, Dec. 10	**1080**	2p Sheet of 8, #a-h	☐	☐	☐	☐
2001, Dec. 10	**1081**	8p shown	☐	☐	☐	☐
2002, Jan. 28	**1082**	5.50p multi	☐	☐	☐	☐
2002, Jan. 28	**1083**	10p multi	☐	☐	☐	☐
2002, Mar. 1	**1084**	2p Block of 6, #a-f	☐	☐	☐	☐
2002, Mar. 1	**1085**	8p multi	☐	☐	☐	☐
2002, Mar. 15	**1086**	Block of 4, #a-d	☐	☐	☐	☐
2002, Mar. 15	**1087**	8p multi	☐	☐	☐	☐
2002, Apr. 12	**1088-1089**	Set of 2	☐	☐	☐	☐
2002, Apr. 12	**1090**	8p multi	☐	☐	☐	☐
2002, May 16	**1091**	Horiz. pair, #a-b	☐	☐	☐	☐
2002, June 5	**1092-1100**	Set of 9	☐	☐	☐	☐
2002, July 24	**1101**	Strip or block of 4, #a-d	☐	☐	☐	☐
2002, July 24	**1102**	6p multi	☐	☐	☐	☐
2002, Sept. 13	**1103-1104**	Set of 2	☐	☐	☐	☐
2002, Sept. 26	**1105**	Block of 4, #a-d	☐	☐	☐	☐
2002, Sept. 26	**1106**	7p multi	☐	☐	☐	☐
2002, Oct. 9	**1107**	Block of 4, #a-d	☐	☐	☐	☐
2002, Oct. 9	**1107E**	Souvenir booklet	☐	☐	☐	☐
2002, Oct. 9	**1108**	7p multi	☐	☐	☐	☐
2002, Nov. 22	**1109**	1.50p Block of 6, #a-f	☐	☐	☐	☐
2002, Nov. 22	**1110**	8p multi	☐	☐	☐	☐
2002, Dec. 13	**1111**	2p Sheet of 8, #a-h	☐	☐	☐	☐
2002, Dec. 13	**1112**	8p multi	☐	☐	☐	☐
2003, Jan. 2	**1113**	5.50p multi	☐	☐	☐	☐
2003, Jan. 2	**1113A**	10p multi	☐	☐	☐	☐
2003, Feb. 15	**1114**	Horiz. strip of 4	☐	☐	☐	☐
2003, Feb. 15	**1115**	9p multi	☐	☐	☐	☐

DATE	SCOTT NO.	DESCRIPTION	UNUSED	USED		
Macao						
2003, Mar. 1	**1116**	2p Block of 6, #a-f	☐	☐	☐	☐
2003, Mar. 1	**1117**	8p multi	☐	☐	☐	☐
2003, Mar. 31	**1118-1119**	Set of 2	☐	☐	☐	☐
2003, May 28	**1120**	Block of 4, #a-d	☐	☐	☐	☐
2003, May 28	**1121**	8p multi	☐	☐	☐	☐
2003, June 18	**1122**	Horiz. strip of 4	☐	☐	☐	☐
2003, June 18	**1123**	9p multi	☐	☐	☐	☐
2003, July 30	**1124**	Block of 8	☐	☐	☐	☐
2003, July 30	**1125**	8p multi	☐	☐	☐	☐
2003, Sept. 10	**1126**	2p Sheet of 8, #a-h	☐	☐	☐	☐
2003, Sept. 10	**1127**	8p multi	☐	☐	☐	☐
2003, Oct. 16	**1128**	Pair, #a-b	☐	☐	☐	☐
2003, Oct. 29	**1129**	Sheet of 6, #a-f	☐	☐	☐	☐
2003, Oct. 29	**1130**	12p multi	☐	☐	☐	☐
2003, Dec. 1	**1131**	Block of 4 #a-d	☐	☐	☐	☐
2003, Dec. 1	**1132**	7p multi	☐	☐	☐	☐
2004, Jan. 8	**1133**	5.50p shown	☐	☐	☐	☐
2004, Jan. 8	**1134**	10p Monkey, diff.	☐	☐	☐	☐
2004, Mar. 1	**1135**	2p Sheet of 8, #a-h	☐	☐	☐	☐
2004, Mar. 1	**1136**	8p multi	☐	☐	☐	☐
2004, May 28	**1137**	1.50p Block of 6, #a-f	☐	☐	☐	☐
2004, May 28	**1138**	8p multi	☐	☐	☐	☐
2004, June 30	**1139**	Horiz. strip of 4	☐	☐	☐	☐
2004, June 30	**1140**	9p God, diff.	☐	☐	☐	☐
2004, July 30	**1141-1144**	Set of 4	☐	☐	☐	☐
2004, Aug. 22	**1145-1146**	Set of 2	☐	☐	☐	☐
2004, Aug. 22	**1147**	8p multi	☐	☐	☐	☐
2004, Sept. 2	**1148**	Block of 4, #a-d	☐	☐	☐	☐
2004, Sept. 2	**1149**	9p multi	☐	☐	☐	☐
2004, Oct. 1	**1150**	Block of 4, #a-d	☐	☐	☐	☐
2004, Oct. 1	**1151**	7p multi	☐	☐	☐	☐
2004, Oct. 9	**1152**	Block or strip of 4, #a-d	☐	☐	☐	☐
2004, Oct. 9	**1153**	8p multi	☐	☐	☐	☐
2004, Dec. 1	**1154**	Block of 6, #a-f	☐	☐	☐	☐
2004, Dec. 1	**1155**	8p multi	☐	☐	☐	☐
2004, Dec. 20	**1156**	Horiz. strip of 4	☐	☐	☐	☐
2004, Dec. 20	**1157**	10p multi	☐	☐	☐	☐
2004, Dec. 28	**1158**	8p multi	☐	☐	☐	☐

DATE	SCOTT NO.	DESCRIPTION	UNUSED	USED		
Macao						
2005, Jan. 13	**1159**	5.50p shown	☐	☐	☐	☐
2005, Jan. 13	**1160**	10p Rooster, diff.	☐	☐	☐	☐
2005, Mar. 1	**1161**	Block of 8	☐	☐	☐	☐
2005, Mar. 1	**1162**	8p multi	☐	☐	☐	☐
2005, Mar. 23	**1163-1164**	Set of 2	☐	☐	☐	☐
2005, Mar. 23	**1165**	8p multi	☐	☐	☐	☐
2005, Apr. 15	**1166**	Horiz. strip of 4	☐	☐	☐	☐
2005, Apr. 15	**1167**	8p Public Commercial Assoc. Library	☐	☐	☐	☐
2005, May 8	**1168**	Horiz. strip of 4 + 4 alternating labels	☐	☐	☐	☐
2005, June 10	**1169**	2p Block of 6, #a-f	☐	☐	☐	☐
2005, June 10	**1170**	8p multi	☐	☐	☐	☐
2005, June 28	**1171**	Horiz. strip of 3	☐	☐	☐	☐
2005, June 28	**1172**	8p multi	☐	☐	☐	☐
2005, July 16	**1173**	Block of 4, #a-d	☐	☐	☐	☐
2005, July 16	**1174**	8p multi	☐	☐	☐	☐
2005, Aug. 30	**1175**	Block of 6, #a-f	☐	☐	☐	☐
2005, Aug. 30	**1176**	8p multi	☐	☐	☐	☐
2005, Sept. 2	**1177-1180**	Set of 4	☐	☐	☐	☐
2005, Sept. 2	**1181**	8p multi	☐	☐	☐	☐
2005, Oct. 9	**1182**	Block of 4, #a-d	☐	☐	☐	☐
2005, Oct. 9	**1183**	8p multi	☐	☐	☐	☐
2005, Nov. 16	**1184**	Block of 6, #a-f	☐	☐	☐	☐
2005, Nov. 16	**1185**	8p multi	☐	☐	☐	☐
2006, Jan. 9	**1186**	5.50p multi	☐	☐	☐	☐
2006, Jan. 9	**1187**	10p multi	☐	☐	☐	☐
2006, Feb. 12	**1188**	Horiz. strip of 4	☐	☐	☐	☐
2006, Feb. 12	**1189**	8p multi	☐	☐	☐	☐
2006, Mar. 1	**1190**	Block of 8	☐	☐	☐	☐
2006, Mar. 1	**1191**	8p multi	☐	☐	☐	☐
2006, May 18	**1192**	Block of 8	☐	☐	☐	☐
2006, May 18	**1193**	10p multi	☐	☐	☐	☐
2006, June 9	**1194**	Block of 4	☐	☐	☐	☐
2006, June 28	**1195**	Vert. strip of 5	☐	☐	☐	☐
2006, June 28	**1196**	10p multi	☐	☐	☐	☐
2006, July 28	**1197**	Block of 4, #a-d	☐	☐	☐	☐
2006, July 28	**1198**	10p multi	☐	☐	☐	☐
2006, Sept. 13	**1199**	Block of 4	☐	☐	☐	☐

DATE	SCOTT NO.	DESCRIPTION	UNUSED	USED		
Macao						
2006, Sept. 13	**1200**	10p multi	☐	☐	☐	☐
2006, Sept. 28	**1201**	Horiz. strip of 5	☐	☐	☐	☐
2006, Sept. 28	**1202**	10p multi	☐	☐	☐	☐
2006, Oct. 9	**1203**	2p Sheet of 8, #a-h	☐	☐	☐	☐
2006, Oct. 9	**1204**	10p shown	☐	☐	☐	☐
2006, Nov. 30	**1205-1208**	Set of 4	☐	☐	☐	☐
2006, Nov. 30	**1209**	10p multi	☐	☐	☐	☐
2007, Jan. 8	**1210**	5.50p multi	☐	☐	☐	☐
2007, Jan. 8	**1211**	10p multi	☐	☐	☐	☐
2007, Feb. 3	**1212**	Block of 4, #a-d	☐	☐	☐	☐
2007, Feb. 3	**1213**	8p multi	☐	☐	☐	☐
2007, Mar. 1	**1214**	Block of 8	☐	☐	☐	☐
2007, Mar. 1	**1215**	10p multi	☐	☐	☐	☐
2007, May 8	**1216**	Block of 4, #a-d	☐	☐	☐	☐
2007, May 8	**1217**	10p multi	☐	☐	☐	☐
2007, June 1	**1218-1221**	Set of 4	☐	☐	☐	☐
2007, June 1	**1222**	10p multi	☐	☐	☐	☐
2007, June 1	**1223**	Booklet pane, #1223a-1223d	☐	☐	☐	☐
2007, June 18	**1224**	Block of 6, #a-f	☐	☐	☐	☐
2007, June 18	**1225**	10p multi	☐	☐	☐	☐
2007, July 9	**1226-1230**	Set of 5	☐	☐	☐	☐
2007, July 9	**1231**	10p multi	☐	☐	☐	☐
2007, Sept. 28	**1232-1233**	Set of 2	☐	☐	☐	☐
2007, Oct. 9	**1234**	10p multi	☐	☐	☐	☐
2007, Oct. 26	**1235**	Block of 4, #a-d	☐	☐	☐	☐
2007, Oct. 26	**1236**	10p multi	☐	☐	☐	☐
2007, Nov. 30	**1237**	Block of 4, #a-d	☐	☐	☐	☐
2007, Nov. 30	**1238**	10p multi	☐	☐	☐	☐
2008, Jan. 23	**1239**	Horiz. strip of 5	☐	☐	☐	☐
2008, Jan. 23	**1240**	10p multi	☐	☐	☐	☐
2008, Mar. 1	**1241**	2p Sheet of 8, #a-h	☐	☐	☐	☐
2008, Mar. 1	**1242**	10p multi	☐	☐	☐	☐
2008, May 3	**1243-1244**	Set of 2	☐	☐	☐	☐
2008, May 3	**1245**	10p multi	☐	☐	☐	☐
2008, June 2	**1246**	Horiz. strip of 4	☐	☐	☐	☐
2008, June 2	**1247**	10p multi	☐	☐	☐	☐
2008, July 4	**1248**	Block of 8	☐	☐	☐	☐

DATE	SCOTT NO.	DESCRIPTION	UNUSED	USED		
Macao						
2008, July 4	**1249**	Sheet of 2	☐	☐	☐	☐
2008, July 31	**1250**	1.50p multi	☐	☐	☐	☐
2008, July 31	**1251**	2p multi	☐	☐	☐	☐
2008, July 31	**1252**	2.50p multi	☐	☐	☐	☐
2008, July 31	**1253**	3p multi	☐	☐	☐	☐
2008, July 31	**1254**	3.50p multi	☐	☐	☐	☐
2008, July 31	**1255**	4p multi	☐	☐	☐	☐
2008, July 31	**1256**	4.50p multi	☐	☐	☐	☐
2008, July 31	**1257**	5p multi	☐	☐	☐	☐
2008, Aug. 8	**1258**	5p multi	☐	☐	☐	☐
2008, Aug. 8	**1259**	10p multi	☐	☐	☐	☐
2008, Oct. 1	**1260**	Sheet of 4, #a-d	☐	☐	☐	☐
2008, Oct. 1	**1261**	10p shown	☐	☐	☐	☐
2008, Oct. 9	**1262**	Horiz. pair, #a-b	☐	☐	☐	☐
2008, Nov. 7	**1263**	10p multi	☐	☐	☐	☐
2008, Dec. 1	**1264-1267**	Set of 4	☐	☐	☐	☐
2008, Dec. 1	**1268**	10p multi	☐	☐	☐	☐
2009, Jan. 4	**1269**	5p black	☐	☐	☐	☐
2009, Jan. 8	**1270**	Horiz. strip of 5	☐	☐	☐	☐
2009, Jan. 8	**1271**	10p multi	☐	☐	☐	☐
2009, Feb. 20	**1272**	Horiz. strip of 4	☐	☐	☐	☐
2009, Feb. 20	**1273**	10p multi	☐	☐	☐	☐
2009, Mar. 1	**1274-1277**	Set of 4	☐	☐	☐	☐
2009, Mar. 1	**1278**	10p multi	☐	☐	☐	☐
2009, Apr. 8	**1279**	10p multi	☐	☐	☐	☐
2009, May 1	**1280-1281**	Set of 2	☐	☐	☐	☐
2009, May 1	**1282**	10p multi	☐	☐	☐	☐
2009, June 1	**1283**	1.50p multi	☐	☐	☐	☐
2009, June 1	**1284**	1.50p multi	☐	☐	☐	☐
2009, June 1	**1285**	3.50p multi	☐	☐	☐	☐
2009, June 1	**1286**	3.50p multi	☐	☐	☐	☐
2009, June 1	**1287**	10p multi	☐	☐	☐	☐
2009, June 1	**1288**	1.50p multi	☐	☐	☐	☐
2009, June 1	**1289**	1.50p multi	☐	☐	☐	☐
2009, June 1	**1290**	3.50p multi	☐	☐	☐	☐
2009, June 1	**1291**	3.50p multi	☐	☐	☐	☐
2009, Oct. 1	**1292**	Block of 4, #a-d	☐	☐	☐	☐
2009, Oct. 1	**1293**	10p multi	☐	☐	☐	☐

DATE	SCOTT NO.	DESCRIPTION	UNUSED	USED		
Macao						
2009, Oct. 9	**1294-1295**	Set of 2	☐	☐	☐	☐
2009, Nov. 29	**1296**	Block or strip of 4, #a-d	☐	☐	☐	☐
2009, Nov. 29	**1297**	10p multi	☐	☐	☐	☐
2009, Dec. 19	**1298**	Block or strip of 4, #a-d	☐	☐	☐	☐
2009, Dec. 19	**1299**	10p multi	☐	☐	☐	☐
2009, Dec. 20	**1300**	Block of 6	☐	☐	☐	☐
2009, Dec. 20	**1301**	10p multi	☐	☐	☐	☐
2009, Dec. 20	**1302**	Horiz. strip of 3	☐	☐	☐	☐
2009, Dec. 20	**1303**	10p multi	☐	☐	☐	☐
2010, Jan. 2	**1304**	Horiz. strip of 5	☐	☐	☐	☐
2010, Jan. 2	**1305**	10p multi	☐	☐	☐	☐
2010, Mar. 1	**1306**	2p Sheet of 8, #a-h	☐	☐	☐	☐
2010, Mar. 1	**1307**	10p multi	☐	☐	☐	☐
2010, Mar. 8	**1308**	Block of 4, #a-d	☐	☐	☐	☐
2010, Mar. 8	**1309**	10p multi	☐	☐	☐	☐
2010, May 1	**1310-1311**	Set of 2	☐	☐	☐	☐
2010, May 1	**1312**	10p multi	☐	☐	☐	☐
2010, June 21	**1313**	Block of 4, #a-d	☐	☐	☐	☐
2010, June 21	**1314**	10p multi	☐	☐	☐	☐
2010, July 15	**1315**	Block of 4, #a-d	☐	☐	☐	☐
2010, July 15	**1316**	10p multi	☐	☐	☐	☐
2010, Aug. 30	**1317**	5.50p multi	☐	☐	☐	☐
2010, Aug. 30	**1318**	10p multi	☐	☐	☐	☐
2010, Sept. 7	**1319**	Block or strip of 4, #a-d	☐	☐	☐	☐
2010, Sept. 7	**1320**	10p multi	☐	☐	☐	☐
2010, Sept. 1	**1321**	Block or strip of 4, #a-d	☐	☐	☐	☐
2010, Sept. 1	**1322**	10d multi	☐	☐	☐	☐
2010, Nov. 5	**1323-1326**	Set of 4	☐	☐	☐	☐
2010, Nov. 5	**1327**	10p multi	☐	☐	☐	☐
2010, Nov. 30	**1328**	Block of 4, #a-d	☐	☐	☐	☐
2010, Nov. 30	**1329**	10p multi	☐	☐	☐	☐
2010, Dec. 18	**1330-1331**	Set of 2	☐	☐	☐	☐
2010, Dec. 18	**1332**	10p multi	☐	☐	☐	☐
2011, Jan. 5	**1333**	Horiz. strip of 5	☐	☐	☐	☐
2011, Jan. 5	**1334**	10p multi	☐	☐	☐	☐
2011, Mar. 1	**1335**	10p multi	☐	☐	☐	☐
2011, Apr. 19	**1336-1339**	Set of 4	☐	☐	☐	☐
2011, May 30	**1340**	Block of 4, #a-d	☐	☐	☐	☐

DATE	SCOTT NO.	DESCRIPTION	UNUSED	USED		
Macao						
2011, May 30	**1341**	10p multi	☐	☐	☐	☐
2011, July 28	**1342**	Block of 6, #a-f	☐	☐	☐	☐
2011, July 28	**1343**	10p multi	☐	☐	☐	☐
2011, Sept. 11	**1344**	Block of 4, #a-d	☐	☐	☐	☐
2011, Oct. 9	**1345**	Block or strip of 4, #a-d	☐	☐	☐	☐
2011, Oct. 9	**1346**	10p multi	☐	☐	☐	☐
2011, Oct. 9	**1347**	Block or strip of 4, #a-d	☐	☐	☐	☐
2011, Oct. 9	**1348**	10p multi	☐	☐	☐	☐
2011, Oct. 10	**1349**	Block or strip of 4, #a-d	☐	☐	☐	☐
2011, Oct. 10	**1350**	10p multi	☐	☐	☐	☐
2011, Oct. 28	**1351-1354**	Set of 4	☐	☐	☐	☐
2011, Oct. 28	**1355**	10p multi	☐	☐	☐	☐
2012, Jan. 5	**1356**	Horiz. strip of 5	☐	☐	☐	☐
2012, Jan. 5	**1357**	12p multi	☐	☐	☐	☐
2012, Jan. 31	**1358-1359**	Set of 2	☐	☐	☐	☐
2012, Mar. 1	**1360**	2p Sheet of 8, #a-h	☐	☐	☐	☐
2012, Mar. 1	**1361**	10p multi	☐	☐	☐	☐
2012, Mar. 28	**1362-1365**	Set of 4	☐	☐	☐	☐
2012, Mar. 28	**1366**	10p multi	☐	☐	☐	☐
2012, May 18	**1367**	Horiz. strip of 4	☐	☐	☐	☐
2012, May 18	**1368**	10p multi	☐	☐	☐	☐
2012, June 10	**1369**	Block of 4, #a-d	☐	☐	☐	☐
2012, June 10	**1370**	10p multi	☐	☐	☐	☐
2012, Aug. 8	**1371**	Block of 4, #a-d	☐	☐	☐	☐
2012, Aug. 8	**1372**	10p multi	☐	☐	☐	☐
2012, Aug. 23	**1373**	Block of 6, #a-f	☐	☐	☐	☐
2012, Aug. 23	**1374**	10p multi	☐	☐	☐	☐
2012, Sept. 20	**1375-1376**	Set of 2	☐	☐	☐	☐
2012, Sept. 21	**1377**	Block of 4, #a-d	☐	☐	☐	☐
2012, Sept. 21	**1378**	10p multi	☐	☐	☐	☐
2012, Oct. 9	**1379**	5p multi	☐	☐	☐	☐
2012, Nov. 30	**1380**	Block of 6, #a-f	☐	☐	☐	☐
2012, Nov. 30	**1381**	12p multi	☐	☐	☐	☐
2013, Jan. 3	**1382**	Horiz. strip of 5	☐	☐	☐	☐
2013, Jan. 3	**1383**	12p multi	☐	☐	☐	☐
2013, Jan. 23	**1384**	Block of 4, #a-d	☐	☐	☐	☐
2013, Jan. 23	**1385**	12p multi	☐	☐	☐	☐
2013, Mar. 1	**1386**	12p multi	☐	☐	☐	☐

DATE	SCOTT NO.	DESCRIPTION	UNUSED	USED		
Macao						
2013, Mar. 31	**1387-1388**	Set of 2	☐	☐	☐	☐
2013, Apr. 25	**1389**	Block of 4, #a-d	☐	☐	☐	☐
2013, Apr. 25	**1390**	12p multi	☐	☐	☐	☐
2013, May 10	**1391**	Block of 4, #a-d	☐	☐	☐	☐
2013, May 10	**1392**	12p multi	☐	☐	☐	☐
2013, June 25	**1393**	Block of 4, #a-d	☐	☐	☐	☐
2013, June 25	**1394**	12p multi	☐	☐	☐	☐
2013, Sept. 13	**1395**	Block of 4, #a-d	☐	☐	☐	☐
2013, Sept. 13	**1396**	12p multi	☐	☐	☐	☐
2013, Oct. 9	**1397**	Block of 4, #a-d	☐	☐	☐	☐
2013, Oct. 9	**1398**	12p multi	☐	☐	☐	☐
2013, Oct. 21	**1399-1400**	Set of 2	☐	☐	☐	☐
2013, Oct. 21	**1401**	12p multi	☐	☐	☐	☐
2013, Nov. 1	**1402**	2p Block of 6, #a-f	☐	☐	☐	☐
2013, Nov. 1	**1403**	12p multi	☐	☐	☐	☐
2013, Nov. 8	**1404**	2p Block of 6, #a-f	☐	☐	☐	☐
2013, Nov. 8	**1405**	12p multi	☐	☐	☐	☐
2013, Nov. 23	**1406-1407**	Set of 2	☐	☐	☐	☐
2014, Jan. 3	**1408**	Horiz. strip of 5	☐	☐	☐	☐
2014, Jan. 3	**1409**	12p multi	☐	☐	☐	☐
2014, Jan. 6	**1410-1413**	Set of 4	☐	☐	☐	☐
2014, Jan. 6	**1414**	12p multi	☐	☐	☐	☐
2014, Mar. 1	**1415**	Block or strip of 4, #a-d	☐	☐	☐	☐
2014, Mar. 1	**1416**	12p multi	☐	☐	☐	☐
2014, Mar. 1	**1417**	50p multi	☐	☐	☐	☐
2014, Apr. 28	**1418**	Block or strip of 4, #a-d	☐	☐	☐	☐
2014, Apr. 28	**1419**	12p multi	☐	☐	☐	☐
2014, June 26	**1420**	2p Block of 6, #a-f	☐	☐	☐	☐
2014, June 26	**1421**	12p multi	☐	☐	☐	☐
2014, Sept. 5	**1422**	2p Block or strip of 4, #a-d	☐	☐	☐	☐
2014, Sept. 5	**1423**	12p multi	☐	☐	☐	☐
2014, Oct. 9	**1424**	Sheet of 6, #a-f, + 3 labels	☐	☐	☐	☐
2014, Oct. 9	**1425**	12p multi	☐	☐	☐	☐
2014, Nov. 1	**1426**	5.50p Horiz. pair, #a-b	☐	☐	☐	☐
2014, Nov. 5	**1427**	2p Block of 4, #a-d	☐	☐	☐	☐
2014, Nov. 5	**1428**	12p multi	☐	☐	☐	☐
2014, Nov. 12	**1429**	Block of 4, #a-d	☐	☐	☐	☐
2014, Nov. 12	**1430**	12p multi	☐	☐	☐	☐

Macao

DATE	SCOTT NO.	DESCRIPTION	UNUSED	USED		
2014, Dec. 20	**1431**	2p Block of 4, #a-d	☐	☐	☐	☐
2014, Dec. 20	**1432**	12p multi	☐	☐	☐	☐
2014, Dec. 20	**1433**	2p Block of 6, #a-f	☐	☐	☐	☐
2014, Dec. 20	**1434**	12p multi	☐	☐	☐	☐
2015, Jan. 5	**1435**	Horiz. strip of 5	☐	☐	☐	☐
2015, Jan. 5	**1436**	12p multi	☐	☐	☐	☐
2015, Feb. 16	**1437**	5.50p multi	☐	☐	☐	☐
2015, Feb. 16	**1438**	12p multi	☐	☐	☐	☐
2015, Mar. 1	**1439**	12p multi	☐	☐	☐	☐
2015, Apr. 27	**1440**	5.50p multi	☐	☐	☐	☐
2015, May 5	**1441**	Block or strip of 4, #a-d	☐	☐	☐	☐
2015, May 5	**1442**	12p multi	☐	☐	☐	☐
2015, June 13	**1443**	Horiz. strip of 4	☐	☐	☐	☐
2015, June 13	**1444**	12p multi	☐	☐	☐	☐
2015, July 8	**1445-1446**	Set of 2	☐	☐	☐	☐
2015, July 8	**1447**	12p multi	☐	☐	☐	☐
2015, July 15	**1448**	Block or strip of 4, #a-d	☐	☐	☐	☐
2015, July 15	**1449**	12p multi	☐	☐	☐	☐
2015, July 31	**1450**	Block of 4, #a-d	☐	☐	☐	☐
2015, July 31	**1451**	12p multi	☐	☐	☐	☐
2015, Sept. 3	**1452-1453**	Set of 2	☐	☐	☐	☐
2015, Sept. 22	**1454-1461**	Set of 8	☐	☐	☐	☐
2015, Oct. 9	**1462**	Horiz. pair, #a-b	☐	☐	☐	☐
2015, Oct. 30	**1463**	2p Block of 6, #a-f	☐	☐	☐	☐
2015, Oct. 30	**1464**	12p multi	☐	☐	☐	☐
2015, Nov. 12	**1465**	Sheet of 3, #a-c, + 6 labels	☐	☐	☐	☐
2015, Nov. 12	**1466**	12p multi	☐	☐	☐	☐
2015, Nov. 30	**1467**	Block of 4, #a-d	☐	☐	☐	☐
2015, Dec. 10	**1468**	Sheet of 9	☐	☐	☐	☐
2015, Dec. 10	**1469**	Booklet pane of 9	☐	☐	☐	☐
2016, Jan. 22	**1470**	Horiz. strip of 5	☐	☐	☐	☐
2016, Jan. 22	**1471**	12p multi	☐	☐	☐	☐
2016, Mar. 1	**1472**	Block or strip of 4, #a-d	☐	☐	☐	☐
2016, Mar. 1	**1473**	12p multi	☐	☐	☐	☐
2016, Mar. 14	**1474**	Block or strip of 4, #a-d	☐	☐	☐	☐
2016, Mar. 14	**1475**	12p multi	☐	☐	☐	☐
2016, Apr. 8	**1476**	Horiz. strip of 4	☐	☐	☐	☐
2016, Apr. 8	**1477**	12p multi	☐	☐	☐	☐

DATE	SCOTT NO.	DESCRIPTION	UNUSED	USED		
Macao						
2016, Apr. 28	**1478**	Block or strip of 4, #a-d	☐	☐	☐	☐
2016, Apr. 28	**1479**	12p multi	☐	☐	☐	☐
2016, May 18	**1480**	Block of 4, #a-d	☐	☐	☐	☐
2016, May 18	**1481**	12p multi	☐	☐	☐	☐
2016, June 17	**1482**	Horiz. pair, #a-b	☐	☐	☐	☐
2016, June 17	**1483**	12p multi	☐	☐	☐	☐
2016, July 29	**1484**	Block of 4, #a-d	☐	☐	☐	☐
2016, July 11	**1485**	2p Sheet of 9, #a-i	☐	☐	☐	☐
2016, Aug. 25	**1486**	Block of 6, #a-f	☐	☐	☐	☐
2016, Aug. 25	**1487**	12p multi	☐	☐	☐	☐
2016, Sept. 10	**1488-1489**	Set of 2	☐	☐	☐	☐
2016, Sept. 10	**1490**	12p multi	☐	☐	☐	☐
2016, Oct. 9	**1491**	Block or horiz. strip of 4, #a-d	☐	☐	☐	☐
2016, Oct. 9	**1492**	12p multi	☐	☐	☐	☐
2016, Nov. 12	**1493**	Block or strip of 4, #a-d	☐	☐	☐	☐
2016, Nov. 12	**1494**	12p multi	☐	☐	☐	☐
2016, Nov. 18	**1495**	Block or strip of 4, #a-d	☐	☐	☐	☐
2016, Nov. 18	**1496**	12p multi	☐	☐	☐	☐
2016, Dec. 1	**1497**	Block of 8, #a-h	☐	☐	☐	☐
2016, Dec. 1	**1498**	12p multi	☐	☐	☐	☐
2017, Jan. 5	**1499**	Horiz. strip of 5	☐	☐	☐	☐
2017, Jan. 5	**1500**	12p multi	☐	☐	☐	☐
2017, Feb. 10	**1501**	Block or strip of 4, #a-d	☐	☐	☐	☐
2017, Feb. 10	**1502**	12p multi	☐	☐	☐	☐
2017, Mar. 1	**1503**	Horiz. strip of 3	☐	☐	☐	☐
2017, June 8	**1504**	Block of 4, #a-d	☐	☐	☐	☐
2017, June 8	**1505**	12p multi	☐	☐	☐	☐
2017, July 3	**1506**	Block of 4, #a-d	☐	☐	☐	☐
2017, July 3	**1507**	12p multi	☐	☐	☐	☐
2017, Aug. 1	**1508**	Block of 6, #a-f	☐	☐	☐	☐
2017, Aug. 1	**1509**	12p multi	☐	☐	☐	☐
2017, Aug. 8	**1510**	Horiz. strip of 4, #a-d	☐	☐	☐	☐
2017, Aug. 8	**1511**	12p multi	☐	☐	☐	☐
2017, Sept. 7	**1512-1513**	Set of 2	☐	☐	☐	☐
2017, Sept. 7	**1514**	12p multi	☐	☐	☐	☐
2017, Oct. 9	**1515**	Block of 4, #a-d	☐	☐	☐	☐
2017, Oct. 9	**1516**	12p multi	☐	☐	☐	☐

DATE	SCOTT NO.	DESCRIPTION	UNUSED	USED		
Macao						
2017, Nov. 10	**1517**	Block of 4, #a-d	☐	☐	☐	☐
2017, Nov. 10	**1518**	12p multi	☐	☐	☐	☐
2017, Nov. 21	**1519**	Sheet of 7, #a-g	☐	☐	☐	☐
2017, Dec. 1	**1520**	Block of 4, #a-d	☐	☐	☐	☐
2018, Jan. 5	**1521**	Horiz. strip of 5	☐	☐	☐	☐
2018, Jan. 5	**1522**	12p multi	☐	☐	☐	☐
2018, Mar. 1	**1523**	Horiz. strip of 3, #a-c	☐	☐	☐	☐
2018, Mar. 1	**1524**	12p multi	☐	☐	☐	☐
2018, Apr. 12	**1525**	12p multi	☐	☐	☐	☐
2018, May 30	**1526**	Block of 4, #a-d	☐	☐	☐	☐
2018, May 30	**1527**	12p multi	☐	☐	☐	☐
2018, June 26	**1528**	Horiz. pair, #a-b	☐	☐	☐	☐
2018, July 6	**1529**	Block of 4, #a-d	☐	☐	☐	☐
2018, July 6	**1530**	12p multi	☐	☐	☐	☐
2018, July 27	**1531**	Block of 4, #a-d	☐	☐	☐	☐
2018, July 27	**1532**	12p multi	☐	☐	☐	☐
2018, Aug. 15	**1533**	Block of 4, #a-d	☐	☐	☐	☐
2018, Aug. 15	**1534**	12p multi	☐	☐	☐	☐
2018, Sept. 23	**1535**	Block of 4, #a-d	☐	☐	☐	☐
2018, Sept. 23	**1536**	12p multi	☐	☐	☐	☐
2018, Oct. 9	**1537**	Block of 4, #a-d	☐	☐	☐	☐
2018, Oct. 9	**1538**	12p multi	☐	☐	☐	☐
2018, Oct. 12	**1539-1540**	Set of 2	☐	☐	☐	☐
2018, Oct. 12	**1541**	12p multi	☐	☐	☐	☐
2018, Oct. 30	**1542**	Horiz. strip of 3	☐	☐	☐	☐
2018, Oct. 30	**1543**	12p multi	☐	☐	☐	☐
2018, Nov. 15	**1544**	Block of 6, #a-f	☐	☐	☐	☐
2019, Jan. 5	**1545**	Horiz. strip of 5	☐	☐	☐	☐
2019, Jan. 5	**1546**	12p multi	☐	☐	☐	☐
2019, Mar. 1	**1547-1548**	Set of 2	☐	☐	☐	☐
2019, Mar. 1	**1549**	50p gold & multi	☐	☐	☐	☐
2019, Mar. 25	**1550**	Horiz. pair, #a-b	☐	☐	☐	☐
2019, Mar. 25	**1551**	12p gold & multi	☐	☐	☐	☐
2019, May 3	**1552**	Block of 4, #a-d	☐	☐	☐	☐
2019, May 3	**1553**	12p multi	☐	☐	☐	☐
2019, May 15	**1554**	Block or strip of 4, #a-d	☐	☐	☐	☐
2019, May 15	**1555**	12p multi	☐	☐	☐	☐
2019, June 3	**1556**	Horiz. strip of 3, #a-c	☐	☐	☐	☐

DATE	SCOTT NO.	DESCRIPTION	UNUSED	USED		
Macao						
2019, June 3	**1557**	12p multi	☐	☐	☐	☐
2019, July 26	**1558**	Block of 4, #a-d	☐	☐	☐	☐
2019, July 26	**1559**	12p silver & multi	☐	☐	☐	☐
2019, Aug. 30	**1560**	Block or strip of 4, #a-d	☐	☐	☐	☐
2019, Aug. 30	**1561**	12p multi	☐	☐	☐	☐
2019, Sept. 13	**1562-1563**	Set of 2	☐	☐	☐	☐
2019, Sept. 13	**1564**	12p multi	☐	☐	☐	☐
2019, Sept. 26	**1565**	Block or strip of 4, #a-d	☐	☐	☐	☐
2019, Sept. 26	**1566**	12p multi	☐	☐	☐	☐
2019, Oct. 1	**1567**	Block or strip of 4, #a-d	☐	☐	☐	☐
2019, Oct. 1	**1568**	12p multi	☐	☐	☐	☐
2019, Oct. 9	**1569**	Block or strip of 4, #a-d	☐	☐	☐	☐
2019, Oct. 9	**1570**	12p multi	☐	☐	☐	☐
2019, Oct. 18	**1571**	Horiz. strip of 3, #a-c	☐	☐	☐	☐
2019, Oct. 18	**1572**	12p multi	☐	☐	☐	☐
2019, Nov. 22	**1573**	2.50p multi	☐	☐	☐	☐
2019, Nov. 22	**1574**	3p multi	☐	☐	☐	☐
2019, Nov. 22	**1575**	3.50p multi	☐	☐	☐	☐
2019, Nov. 22	**1576**	4p multi	☐	☐	☐	☐
2019, Nov. 22	**1577**	4.50p multi	☐	☐	☐	☐
2019, Nov. 22	**1578**	5p multi	☐	☐	☐	☐
2019, Nov. 22	**1579**	5.50p multi	☐	☐	☐	☐
2019, Nov. 22	**1580**	6p multi	☐	☐	☐	☐
2019, Dec. 10	**1581-1582**	Set of 2	☐	☐	☐	☐
2019, Dec. 10	**1583**	12p multi	☐	☐	☐	☐
2019, Dec. 20	**1584**	Block of 4, #a-d	☐	☐	☐	☐
2019, Dec. 20	**1585**	12p multi	☐	☐	☐	☐
2019, Dec. 20	**1586**	Sheet of 6, #1586a-1586c, People's Republic of China #4692-4697	☐	☐	☐	☐
2019, Dec. 20	**1587**	Block of 6, #a-f	☐	☐	☐	☐
2019, Dec. 20	**1588**	12p multi	☐	☐	☐	☐
2020, Jan. 5	**1589**	Block of 4, #a-d	☐	☐	☐	☐
2020, Jan. 5	**1590**	14p multi	☐	☐	☐	☐
2020, Jan. 20	**1591**	Block of 4, #a-d	☐	☐	☐	☐
2020, Jan. 20	**1592**	14p multi	☐	☐	☐	☐
2020, Mar. 1	**1593**	Block of 4, #a-d	☐	☐	☐	☐
2020, Mar. 1	**1594**	14p multi	☐	☐	☐	☐
2020, Apr. 20	**1595**	Block or strip of 4, #a-d	☐	☐	☐	☐

DATE	SCOTT NO.	DESCRIPTION	UNUSED	USED		
Macao						
2020, Apr. 20	**1596**	14p multi	☐	☐	☐	☐
2020, May 21	**1597-1600**	Set of 4	☐	☐	☐	☐
2020, May 21	**1601**	14p multi	☐	☐	☐	☐
2020, June 12	**1602**	4.50p gold & multi	☐	☐	☐	☐
2020, June 12	**1603**	14p gold & multi	☐	☐	☐	☐
2020, June 24	**1604**	2.50p multi	☐	☐	☐	☐
2020, June 24	**1605**	14p multi	☐	☐	☐	☐
2020, July 3	**1606**	Block of 4, #a-d	☐	☐	☐	☐
2020, July 3	**1607**	14p multi	☐	☐	☐	☐
2020, Aug. 10	**1608**	Block or strip of 4, #a-d	☐	☐	☐	☐
2020, Aug. 10	**1609**	14p multi	☐	☐	☐	☐
2020, Sept. 10	**1610**	Block or strip of 4, #a-d	☐	☐	☐	☐
2020, Sept. 10	**1611**	14p multi	☐	☐	☐	☐
2020, Sept. 28	**1612**	Block of 4, #a-d	☐	☐	☐	☐
2020, Sept. 28	**1613**	14p multi	☐	☐	☐	☐
2020, Oct. 9	**1614**	Block of 4, #a-d	☐	☐	☐	☐
2020, Oct. 9	**1615**	14p multi	☐	☐	☐	☐
2020, Oct. 30	**1616**	Block or strip of 4, #a-d	☐	☐	☐	☐
2020, Oct. 30	**1617**	14p multi	☐	☐	☐	☐
2020, Nov. 30	**1618**	Sheet of 6, #a-f	☐	☐	☐	☐
2020, Nov. 30	**1619**	14p multi	☐	☐	☐	☐
2020, Dec. 16	**1620**	Horiz. pair, #a-b	☐	☐	☐	☐
2020, Dec. 16	**1621**	14p multi	☐	☐	☐	☐
2021, Jan. 5	**1622**	Block of 4, #a-d	☐	☐	☐	☐
2021, Jan. 5	**1623**	14p multi	☐	☐	☐	☐
2021, Feb. 22	**1624**	Horiz. pair, #a-b	☐	☐	☐	☐
2021, Feb. 22	**1625**	14p multi	☐	☐	☐	☐
2012, Oct. 9	**B1**	Horiz. pair, #a-b	☐	☐	☐	☐
1936	**C1**	2a blue green	☐	☐	☐	☐
1936	**C2**	3a violet	☐	☐	☐	☐
1936	**C3**	5a on 6a brown	☐	☐	☐	☐
1936	**C4**	7a brt rose	☐	☐	☐	☐
1936	**C5**	8a brt blue	☐	☐	☐	☐
1936	**C6**	15a maroon	☐	☐	☐	☐
1938, Aug. 1	**C7**	1a scarlet	☐	☐	☐	☐
1938, Aug. 1	**C8**	2a purple	☐	☐	☐	☐
1938, Aug. 1	**C9**	3a orange	☐	☐	☐	☐
1938, Aug. 1	**C10**	5a ultra	☐	☐	☐	☐

DATE	SCOTT NO.	DESCRIPTION	UNUSED	USED		
Macao						
1938, Aug. 1	**C11**	10a lilac brn	☐	☐	☐	☐
1938, Aug. 1	**C12**	20a dk green	☐	☐	☐	☐
1938, Aug. 1	**C13**	50a red brown	☐	☐	☐	☐
1938, Aug. 1	**C14**	70a rose car	☐	☐	☐	☐
1938, Aug. 1	**C15**	1p magenta	☐	☐	☐	☐
1960, Dec. 11	**C16**	50a shown	☐	☐	☐	☐
1960, Dec. 11	**C17**	76a Penha Chapel	☐	☐	☐	☐
1960, Dec. 11	**C18**	3p Macao	☐	☐	☐	☐
1960, Dec. 11	**C19**	5p Bairro de Mong Ha	☐	☐	☐	☐
1960, Dec. 11	**C20**	10p Penha and Bay	☐	☐	☐	☐
1979, Aug. 3	**C21**	70a on 76a multi	☐	☐	☐	☐
1904, July	**J1**	1/2a gray green	☐	☐	☐	☐
1904, July	**J2**	1a yellow grn	☐	☐	☐	☐
1904, July	**J3**	2a slate	☐	☐	☐	☐
1904, July	**J4**	4a pale brown	☐	☐	☐	☐
1904, July	**J5**	5a red orange	☐	☐	☐	☐
1904, July	**J6**	8a gray brown	☐	☐	☐	☐
1904, July	**J7**	12a red brown	☐	☐	☐	☐
1904, July	**J8**	20a dull blue	☐	☐	☐	☐
1904, July	**J9**	40a carmine	☐	☐	☐	☐
1904, July	**J10**	50a orange	☐	☐	☐	☐
1904, July	**J11**	1p gray violet	☐	☐	☐	☐
1911	**J12**	½a gray green	☐	☐	☐	☐
1911	**J13**	1a yellow green	☐	☐	☐	☐
1911	**J14**	2a slate	☐	☐	☐	☐
1911	**J15**	4a pale brown	☐	☐	☐	☐
1911	**J16**	5a orange	☐	☐	☐	☐
1911	**J17**	8a gray brown	☐	☐	☐	☐
1911	**J18**	12a red brown	☐	☐	☐	☐
1911	**J19**	20a dull blue	☐	☐	☐	☐
1911	**J20**	40a carmine (G)	☐	☐	☐	☐
1911	**J21**	50a orange	☐	☐	☐	☐
1911	**J22**	1p gray violet	☐	☐	☐	☐
1914	**J22A**	½a gray green	☐	☐	☐	☐
1914	**J23**	1a yellow green	☐	☐	☐	☐
1914	**J24**	2a slate	☐	☐	☐	☐
1914	**J25**	4a pale brown	☐	☐	☐	☐
1914	**J26**	5a orange	☐	☐	☐	☐

DATE	SCOTT NO.	DESCRIPTION	UNUSED	USED		
Macao						
1914	**J27**	8a gray brown	☐	☐	☐	☐
1914	**J28**	12a red brown	☐	☐	☐	☐
1914	**J29**	20a dull blue	☐	☐	☐	☐
1914	**J30**	40a car (G)	☐	☐	☐	☐
1914	**J31**	50a orange	☐	☐	☐	☐
1914	**J32**	1p gray violet	☐	☐	☐	☐
1947	**J33**	1a red violet	☐	☐	☐	☐
1947	**J34**	2a purple	☐	☐	☐	☐
1947	**J35**	4a dark blue	☐	☐	☐	☐
1947	**J36**	5a chocolate	☐	☐	☐	☐
1947	**J37**	8a red violet	☐	☐	☐	☐
1947	**J38**	12a orange brown	☐	☐	☐	☐
1947	**J39**	20a yellow green	☐	☐	☐	☐
1947	**J40**	40a brt carmine	☐	☐	☐	☐
1947	**J41**	50a orange yellow	☐	☐	☐	☐
1947	**J42**	1p blue	☐	☐	☐	☐
1949, May 1	**J43**	1a on 4a black	☐	☐	☐	☐
1949, May 1	**J44**	2a on 6a brown	☐	☐	☐	☐
1949, May 1	**J45**	4a on 8a brt blue	☐	☐	☐	☐
1949, May 1	**J46**	5a on 10a red org	☐	☐	☐	☐
1949, May 1	**J47**	8a on 12a dk blue	☐	☐	☐	☐
1949, May 1	**J48**	12a on 30a apple grn	☐	☐	☐	☐
1949, May 1	**J49**	20a on 40a violet	☐	☐	☐	☐
1951, June 6	**J50**	1a org yel, lem	☐	☐	☐	☐
1951, June 6	**J51**	2a dk grn, bl (C)	☐	☐	☐	☐
1951, June 6	**J52**	7a on 10a brt pink, bl	☐	☐	☐	☐
1952	**J53**	1a violet blue	☐	☐	☐	☐
1952	**J54**	3a chocolate	☐	☐	☐	☐
1952	**J55**	5a indigo	☐	☐	☐	☐
1952	**J56**	10a dark red	☐	☐	☐	☐
1952	**J57**	30a indigo	☐	☐	☐	☐
1952	**J58**	1p chocolate	☐	☐	☐	☐
1919, Aug. 11	**MR1**	2a green	☐	☐	☐	☐
1919, Aug. 11	**MR2**	11a green (C)	☐	☐	☐	☐
1892-93	**P1**	2½r on 40r choc	☐	☐	☐	☐
1892-93	**P2**	2½r on 80r gray	☐	☐	☐	☐
1892-93	**P3**	2½r on 10r grn ('93)	☐	☐	☐	☐
1893-94	**P4**	2½r brown	☐	☐	☐	☐

DATE	SCOTT NO.	DESCRIPTION	UNUSED	USED		
Macao						
1893-94	**P5**	½a on 2½r brn (Bk) ('94)	☐	☐	☐	☐
1925, Nov. 3	**RA1**	2a red org & blk	☐	☐	☐	☐
1925, Nov. 3	**RA2**	2a red org & blk	☐	☐	☐	☐
1925, Nov. 3	**RA3**	2a red org & blk	☐	☐	☐	☐
1930, Dec. 25	**RA4**	5a dk brown, yel	☐	☐	☐	☐
1945-47	**RA5**	5a blk brn, yel	☐	☐	☐	☐
1945-47	**RA6**	5a bl, bluish, perf 11x11½ ('47)	☐	☐	☐	☐
1945-47	**RA7**	10a grn, citron	☐	☐	☐	☐
1945-47	**RA8**	15a org, buff	☐	☐	☐	☐
1945-47	**RA9**	20a rose red, sal	☐	☐	☐	☐
1945-47	**RA10**	50a red vio, pnksh, perf 11x11½	☐	☐	☐	☐
1953-56	**RA11**	10a bl, pale grn ('56)	☐	☐	☐	☐
1953-56	**RA12**	20a chocolate, yel	☐	☐	☐	☐
1953-56	**RA13**	50a car, pale rose	☐	☐	☐	☐
1958	**RA14**	1a gray grn, grnsh	☐	☐	☐	☐
1958	**RA15**	2a rose lilac, grysh	☐	☐	☐	☐
1961-66	**RA16**	1a gray grn, grnsh	☐	☐	☐	☐
1961-66	**RA17**	2a rose lil, grysh	☐	☐	☐	☐
1961-66	**RA18**	10a bl, pale grn ('62)	☐	☐	☐	☐
1961-66	**RA19**	20a brn, yel ('66)	☐	☐	☐	☐
1976-79	**RA19A**	20a on 3p blk, brn ('78)	☐	☐	☐	☐
1976-79	**RA19B**	20a on 5p brn, yel	☐	☐	☐	☐
1976-79	**RA20**	20a on 1p yel grn, cream ('79)	☐	☐	☐	☐
1981	**RA20A**	10a on 15a #RA8	☐	☐	☐	☐
1981	**RA21**	20a on 2a #RA17	☐	☐	☐	☐
1925	**RAJ1**	4a red orange & blk	☐	☐	☐	☐
1925	**RAJ2**	4a red orange & blk	☐	☐	☐	☐
1925	**RAJ3**	4a red orange & blk	☐	☐	☐	☐

SCOTT

POSTAGE STAMP

CHECKLIST

Macao

EDITOR-IN-CHIEF .... Jay Bigalke
EDITOR-AT-LARGE .... Donna Houseman
CONTRIBUTING EDITOR .... Charles Snee
EDITOR EMERITUS .... James E. Kloetzel
SENIOR EDITOR/NEW ISSUES & VALUING .... Martin J. Frankevicz
ADMINISTRATIVE ASSISTANT/CATALOGUE LAYOUT .... Eric Wiessinger
PRINTING AND IMAGE COORDINATOR .... Stacey Mahan
SENIOR GRAPHIC DESIGNER .... Cinda McAlexander
ADVERTISING/SALES .... David Pistello, Eric Roth, Brenda Wyen, Julie Dalhstrom
PRESIDENT .... Rick Amos

AMOS MEDIA

1660 Campbell Road, Suite A, Sidney, Ohio 45365

Publishers of
Linn's Stamp News, *Linn's Stamp News Monthly*,
Coin World, and *Coin World Monthly*